KEYS TO DEALING WITH THE LOSS OF A LOVED ONE

Mary K. Kouri, Ph.D.

All inquiries should be addressed to:
Barron's Educational Series, Inc.
250 Wireless Boulevard
Hauppauge, New York 11788

Library of Congress Catalog Card No. 91-10700

International Standard Book No. 0-8120-4676-5

Library of Congress Cataloging in Publication Data

Kouri, Mary K., 1943–.
    Keys to dealing with the loss of a loved one / Mary K. Kouri.
        p.   cm.—(Barron's retirement keys)
    Includes bibliographical references.
    ISBN 0-8120-4676-5
    1. Bereavement—Psychological aspects.   2. Death—Psychological
aspects.   3. Grief.   4. Death.   I. Title.   II. Series.
BF575.G7K65   1991
155.9'37—dc20   91-10700
                                                                        CIP

PRINTED IN THE UNITED STATES OF AMERICA
1234   5500   987654321

CONTENTS

At least, my dear,
You did not have to live to see me die.

—Edna St. Vincent Millay

ACKNOWLEDGMENTS

Thanks to the many people who helped, encouraged, and cheered me on through every step of this project: Yancey Stockwell, dear friend and professional associate, who weathered my swings between jubilation and despondency and took over the cooking sometimes to give me more time at the computer; my friends and family, whose kind words and interest in the book's progress reminded me that there was indeed progress even when I lost sight of it; Lynn Sackman, my editor at Barron's, whose kindness warmed my heart each time we talked and whose encouragement helped me to look at the rough drafts with a more tolerant eye; the librarians at the Denver Public Library's main branch and Ross Cherry Creek branch, for answering my innumerable phone queries and for shuttling stacks of books (often the same books two or three times!) from one location to the other; the well-informed, helpful staff of the Tattered Cover Bookstore, for answering phone queries and giving me rundowns on the latest books; and all of you who shared your time and thoughts through interviews.

INTRODUCTION

This book is short. Don't let that mislead you into believing you've found a quick route through your grief, or that at last you've found the quick fix for someone you love who just can't seem to get over a death.

Instead, as its title suggests, this book is a set of keys. These keys can unlock a door when you summon the courage to use them, the door between you and the fiery pain that rages inside you. Why would you want to unlock that door? Because there is no other way to get through the pain and put it behind you. If you've been straining to hold the door closed or to find a way around it, you probably know by now how the battle saps your vitality. Perhaps you are even paying a toll in depression, emptiness, bitterness, or physical illness.

If you unlock the door to your grief, you may find that it's less frightening face to face than it was when you kept it locked up. Getting through the pain will take as long as it takes. Eventually you'll be better. Try to believe this; it is based on the experiences of millions of people throughout recorded history.

In Part One of this book, we explain the complex range of human responses to the loss of loved ones. Part Two contains an array of practical suggestions for coping with the emotional pain and physical effects of grief. Part Three offers help with the financial and legal matters you may encounter after the death of a loved one. Part Four contains a set of keys on rebuilding your life with fulfilling, productive uses for your time and energy.

Finally, the Appendix contains four sections with resources for further assistance and information keyed to the topics covered in the first four parts of the book. Listed are books, pamphlets, audio and video tapes, and organizations.

May you be surefooted as you journey through this time of your life. Carry the best of your past with you and build your future upon it.

1

THE MANY FACES OF "NORMAL GRIEF"

"Is this normal?" you ask as you encounter the physical and emotional trauma that follow the loss of your loved one. "Sleeplessness, anxiety, fear, intense anger, suicidal ideas, a loss of interest in activity, a preoccupation with self and with sad feelings—you may think these all add up to 'going crazy,' " says Ann Stearns in *Living Through Personal Crisis*. In fact, they are all normal. On the other hand, relief is also normal if death follows a painful or long illness.

Grief comes in three phases. Shock is the first. Some people experience shock as numbness and feel as if they are walking around in a daze. Others deny the reality, thinking or hoping there has been a mistake—"That isn't really Sarah" or "Maybe he is just asleep again." Shock is usually more intense when a death is unexpected. When there is time to anticipate the loss, as with a long illness, shock often hits with full intensity at the news of the illness.

When people are in shock, they may appear to be calm, to be "taking it very well." In fact, they may be pillars of support for others. Shock can take many other forms, including emotional outbursts, explosions of anger, and hysterical sobbing or screaming. Some individuals withdraw into uncharacteristic quietness or confusion. A sense of being outside of one's body observing what is going on and feeling disoriented are common.

After the shock wears off, the second phase of grief—accepting the reality of the loss—sets in. Psychologist

1

Therese Rando describes this as the "painful time when you really, truly learn that your loved one is gone . . . Each pang of grief, each stab of pain you feel whenever your expectation or desire or need to be with that person is unfulfilled, 'teaches' you again that your loved one is no longer here." This phase of mourning affects your emotions, your physical well-being, your mental functioning, and your relationships with others. It can last a year or longer, especially when the death was unexpected.

Feelings are intense, often unpredictable. They can swing from sadness and despair at one moment to crankiness and anger at the next. People who were never "moody" can become so as they grieve. It is common to be afraid that you will never get over the loss. Preoccupation with the deceased, even searching for and having dreams and visions of the person are natural during this time. Confusion and inability to concentrate are normal. When these occur, protect your own safety and that of others by not driving or operating potentially dangerous equipment. Intense bursts or spasms of grief can arise without warning, as when you see a flower your loved one enjoyed, smell a familiar aroma, or hear a favorite tune.

Grief ravages your body as well as your emotions. The following responses are not uncommon: exhaustion, sleeplessness, oversleeping, loss of appetite, nausea, diarrhea, constipation, weakness, nervousness, decreased or increased interest in sex, weight loss or gain, heart palpitations, shortness of breath, uncontrollable weeping, feelings of heaviness, and difficulty in swallowing. One woman reported that she was nauseated and had trouble swallowing solid food for six months after her husband's unexpected death. While these are normal responses to the stress of grief, it's essential to get adequate nutrition, exercise, and medical care to prevent long-term problems.

Sometimes mourning involves a sense of urgency concerning your loved one's belongings. This can be an intense desire to keep everything as it was—clothes, eyeglasses, tools. It can take the opposite turn—the urge to clear out painful reminders as quickly as possible. As your grief subsides, these urges toward extreme action give way to more rational judgments for the long run.

During this painful middle phase of grief, time with friends and relatives can present difficulties. Sometimes the desire to have others around is overwhelming. You may be frightened of being alone, particularly in the weeks immediately after the death and at night. It is also normal to want to be left alone with your thoughts and to be irritated at what seem to be intrusions from others. Sometimes the bereaved resent any mention of the deceased person's shortcomings. They may be offended by humor involving the deceased. Others bring their loved one into every conversation, recollecting the past, reiterating their loneliness and sorrow. This sometimes strains relationships with friends and relatives and may best be done in a grief support group.

The duration of these two most difficult phases of grief depends on many factors. One is the nature of the lost relationship: the part the deceased played in your family and social life, the age at death, the positive and negative qualities of the relationship, the satisfaction you derived from the relationship, your fulfilled and unfulfilled expectations for the relationship, your perception of the quality of your loved one's life, and the number of "secondary" losses the death brings (such as security, income, an intelligent business partner, a pleasant companion, or a close friend).

Other factors that influence the length and depth of pain in mourning include: your coping patterns; your social, religious, and cultural background; your age and sex; and the presence of other stresses. The circumstances of death affect mourning: the timeliness, cause, your perception of the preventability of death, and the opportunity to prepare and say goodbye to your loved one. The support you have from friends, relatives, and professionals; your economic and occupational circumstances; and the quality of the mourning rituals that followed the death can ease or hinder your recovery from grief.

The social acceptability of the relationship and the nature of the death affect the amount of support available to the bereaved and can ease or slow the recovery. For example, the widow of a 40-year marriage can expect more social support for her grief than can the survivors of an habitual offender shot in a gun battle with police, or the mother of a 28-year-old male AIDS victim, or the 20-year lover of a married man, or the survivor of a 35-year same-sex relationship, or the 62-year-old unmarried lover of a 79-year-old widower.

The intense pain of the second phase of grief diminishes as you complete the process of letting go of your loved one. This leads to the third phase of grief, in which you accept that the loss is permanent and start to rebuild your life. As you complete your grief you'll see signs—re-awakening to the pleasures of laughter, social activities, food, art, music, work, hobbies, and nature. Physical energy and the ability to concentrate increase, and renewed interest in living replaces your preoccupation with the death of your loved one.

2

ANTICIPATORY GRIEF

As medical technology advances, lingering illness becomes more common than sudden death. People with cancer, heart problems, emphysema, diabetes, Alzheimer's disease, or strokes frequently live for months or years after a diagnosis is made. For them and their loved ones, the process of mourning begins when they learn of their illness. For some individuals, it begins when they suspect that they are ill prior to a medical confirmation.

This mourning process is called *anticipatory grief.* Often it begins with shock and proceeds to denial. For example, one widow recalled the day she learned of her husband's lung cancer: "I was a zombie, I just kept hearing 'inoperable tumor . . . inoperable tumor.' For several days after that, I would look at him and see the words, like a banner in the air, 'inoperable tumor.' " Then came denial. She ranted at the doctor's insensitivity in painting such a bleak picture. After all, there have been many strides in the treatment of cancer. "While I was in the middle of one of my tirades, my daughter reminded me that this diagnosis came from a specialist and it was a second opinion." After that, she began to face the reality of losing her husband.

Grief over the impending decline and death of someone you love has several dimensions. One is the loss of hope for a future filled with the possibilities and expectations that were realistic when your loved one was healthy and able. Perhaps there were plans for travel or joint projects that you must now cancel. If your relationship was less than you wanted it to be, you may grieve the loss of the time to improve it.

Anticipatory grief involves sorrow and dread at the progressive losses you and your loved one must face. With cancer, for example, you foresee a time when he might lose the strength to walk, to take care of himself, perhaps even the ability to recognize you and others who have been close to him.

You may also flinch at the anticipation of hardships the illness is likely to entail for you, your family, or your friends. You may dread the loneliness of being a caregiver. You may worry that your limited financial resources will not allow for adequate care. If you are losing a spouse who managed the family business or finances, you may be frightened about your capacity to carry out these responsibilities.

For many people, part of anticipatory grief is the struggle over how much of their own lives to set aside in order to attend to their loved one's needs. One woman described her mixed feelings concerning her husband's illness and his need for daily care: "It happened just after I got my catering business off the ground. I felt so guilty that I didn't want to quit and take care of him full time. The children were surprised when I finally decided to continue the business part time. They had always seen me put aside my plans for Charley."

Anger is a normal part of anticipatory grief. The sick person is a common target—"How dare you leave me alone?" "If you had taken better care of yourself as I always told you to . . . " "I didn't want our last year together to be like this." "Just as I'm starting a new phase of my life, you get sick." If the relationship was a difficult one, you may feel angry about the added burden and changes in your life that the illness can bring and that your chances to improve the relationship are now limited.

Guilt is often a part of anticipatory grief. Perhaps there are wrongdoings that you still regret. You might wish you had insisted that he see a doctor sooner, or that you had taken that dream vacation last year. People often feel guilty about their present and past anger toward the sick person.

Before your loved one's death, there is the tension between involvement with, and separation from, him. One the one hand, you might want to cling desperately to the relationship since time is passing. On the other hand, you may tell yourself, "I must get used to the idea that he will be gone."

Conflicts can erupt as family members go through the stages of involvement and separation at different times. Some members remain fiercely involved until the end, as if tenderly hovering over every need will keep the loved one alive. Others detach themselves early, visiting less frequently or keeping conversations impersonal.

Realize that throughout his illness, your loved one faces the task of letting go of life as he has known it. He must reformulate his sense of time and future. He might want to be alone or to have private moments with friends, a minister, other family members, or caring professionals as he prepares for death. He may experience anger, depression, or anxiety as never before. Illness and medications often cause personality changes that make communication and care difficult.

While it is possible, talk with your loved one about his wishes regarding a living will, a durable power of attorney, and life-sustaining measures. If choices are feasible, discuss whether he wants to be at home, in a hospice, nursing home, or hospital.

You can best manage anticipatory grief by honestly talking about your feelings with your loved one, and with friends and family members as well. One widow, Norma Upson, explains in *When Someone You Love Is Dying*, "Sharing sorrow with a loved one when there is to be a final parting can open doors and allow us to say things that are important at the time and vital to survivors after the beloved dies." Regarding anger and frustration, she says, "Vent [them] properly and honestly and you will find that because it *is* natural and normal, you can then deal with [them] without adding to the burden of guilt you'll feel during the after-death grieving process."

It is important to you and your loved one that you release him to die in his own time. Reassure him that he has your affection and that you are confident in his ability to choose what is best for him. One man expressed it in this way to his uncle: "I love you. I'll miss you when you're gone, and I'll always remember you. I trust you to know when it's time to say goodbye to us."

During this stressful time, safeguard your well-being for your own sake and that of your loved one.

Arrange with friends and professionals to share the duties of caregiving. Join a support group for families or caregivers. Tend to your physical health by eating nutritious foods, making time for being outdoors in the sunshine, and getting some exercise. Rejuvinate your spirits by arranging for regular time away. Take a walk with a good friend who will listen supportively to your feelings and concerns. Get a massage. Have dinner with friends who can help you laugh. Keep abreast of your financial affairs.

By tending to your well-being, you can better help your loved one prepare for death while coping with your own grief over your loss.

3

COPING
WITH GUILT

Few people escape guilt as they grieve. In this key, we discuss the kinds of guilt that many people encounter during mourning and suggestions for managing it.

"I should have, could have . . . ," "If only I had known . . . at the time, it would have been different,"—these are the anguished regrets of the mourner who expects of himself superhuman efforts, if not miracles. If you are plagued by such pain, ask yourself this: "Given all the circumstances of the moment, did I act on what I thought was best?" Remember that it is always easier to see what might have been a better course of action as you look back in time. This vantage point usually blurs the impact of fatigue, panic, preoccupation, lack of knowledge, or human error, all of which complicate stressful times.

One widow carried a nagging guilt for a year and a half after her husband's death because she had relied on just one doctor's opinion about the proper course of treatment for her husband's cancer. When she finally took the medical records to an attorney, she learned that the tumor had been untreatable and that her husband could not have lived any longer no matter what the course of treatment. By doing this fact-finding, she freed herself from what Alla Bozarth-Campbell calls in her book, *Life Is Goodbye Life Is Hello: Grieving Well Through All Kinds of Loss,* the "Great Torture of *If.*" She checked the realities of the situation and replaced her frightening "ifs" with facts, allowing her to lay her guilt to rest at last.

Often, when a long or difficult illness precedes death, caretakers anticipate relief from the energy drain, stress, or expense. Then they punish themselves with guilt for having had such thoughts. Sometimes survivors report that they feel guilty at the sense of liberation they have after the funeral when, at long last, they can make plans to rebuild their lives.

Keep in mind that it is normal for human beings to look forward to the end of difficult times in their lives. While few people would plot their own gain at the expense of a loved one, it is important to recognize that life's events are seldom black or white. There is usually a tinge of pain in the most joyous of times, and a glimmer of joy in the darkest hours. Caroline Bird captured this truth as it concerns human relationships when she wrote in her book *The Good Years: Your Life in the Twenty-First Century,* "Nobody realizes how much energy a relationship impounds until it is over."

People wish that others would die for various reasons. At times the wish is actually a desire to see an end to a loved one's suffering. This is often the case when a sick person's suffering is extreme and unrelenting. Another aspect of such a wish is the desire for an end to the pain of your own helplessness in not being able to make the situation better. Sometimes a real and legitimate aspect of such situations is the fear that the illness may drain your financial resources beyond the point of recovery.

In troubled or troublesome relationships, people sometimes wish for the death of the other as they long for peace from the turmoil of the relationship. Survivors sometimes experience guilt from "magical thinking"— the false belief that wishing can make something happen.

If you have such guilt, remind yourself that simply wishing something cannot make it happen. If it could, would you not have improved your relationship with the deceased by wishing? Why could you not use the power of wishing to be better organized, smarter, better looking, thinner, or whatever your heart's desire?

A most painful guilt arises from carelessness, neglect, or deliberate actions that result in harm to another. Perhaps you regret words or actions intended to inflict emotional or physical pain, neglectfulness toward responsibilities you had clearly agreed to carry out, carelessness regarding safety precautions, or driving under the influence of alcohol or other drugs.

If this is your burden, it is crucial that you get help in dealing with it. Enlist a friend, a family member, and or a counselor, who can make it clear to you that you are loved and accepted despite what has happened, advises psychologist Ann Kaiser Stearns in her book *Living Through Personal Crisis*.

Thousands of people throughout history have struggled with such guilt. Many have eased their pain by making retribution through activities or services that help others to prevent such misfortunes in their lives, such as conducting grief support groups, teaching healthy communication methods to families, volunteering services to community groups that work against alcohol abuse or domestic violence, or writing articles from which others can learn without repeating destructive experiences.

In almost all circumstances, it is helpful to talk about the pain of your guilt. Find a compassionate person who will listen without passing judgment and who will nudge you toward passageways through the guilt. As you work through your guilt, you can free your energy for use in healing and rebuilding your life.

4

ANGER AND GRIEF

People get angry whenever something they want is taken away. Anger comes in degrees ranging from a few seconds of irritation when your ballpoint pen runs out of ink as you write a check to deep rage when your new car refuses to start a few days after the warranty expires.

When someone you care about dies, it is natural to be angry about the losses you suffer. Often the anger does not seem to be "rational." For instance, you might be angry with your loved one about the circumstances or timing of his death. Perhaps you are simply angry at him for depriving you of the joy he brought to your life.

When people believe that they should not feel anger in connection with death or that only certain kinds of anger are acceptable, they often cover up or redirect those feelings they think are unacceptable. For example, one widow said she did not realize how angry she was after her husband's death. "Instead, I felt hurt. Then, when I got very angry, I would get sick to my stomach. When my doctor sent me to a class on grief and anger, I learned that I was using the hurt feelings and the physical sickness to cover up my anger," she said.

Sometimes the bereaved adhere closely to the old saw that one should not speak ill of the dead. To heed this directive, they "protect" the deceased by remembering only his positive qualities. In doing this, survivors keep themselves from experiencing and resolving their normal anger over the loss they have suffered. Others redirect their anger by lashing out at convenient targets—family members, a physician, hospital staff, ambulance crew, funeral director, insurance company, God, or fate.

Sometimes people direct their anger inward in self-defeating ways. Signs of this, Stearns writes in *Living Through Personal Crisis*, are depression, accident-proneness, thoughts of suicide, irritability, sleep problems, excessive drinking or eating, and other physical problems. Seldom do mourners *intentionally* turn their anger upon themselves. More often, they are not aware that they are angry, or they suffer guilt or shame since they believe anger to be an unacceptable emotion.

Ironically, anger itself can serve as a mask for other emotions in the mourning process. Just as some individuals do not accept anger in themselves, others do not accept the abject sorrow, unsettling fear, relief, or guilt that they might have. For example, one man raged for more than a decade over the death of his grown daughter in an unsolved murder. A widow resented for years that her friends continued to enjoy their relationships with spouses while she was left alone. Anger that rages or smolders for so long is often a sign of other feelings that have not been faced and put to rest. Dorie Furman, president of a local chapter of the Widowed Persons Service, observes that men are more likely to use anger to avoid the sadness and emptiness of grief, whereas women avoid their anger through sadness and fear.

Anger can be more manageable and less frightening when you remember two things. First, it does not always have a logical justification. You can view anger as a form of energy to use as an aid in moving through your grief. Second, you have choices about the ways you express your anger. Some modes of expression are inappropriate, hurtful, or nonproductive, but others are useful and healthy. According to Furman for example, many individuals find the strength and encouragement to express anger about their losses and pain when they are surrounded by the caring and acceptance of support groups; eventually they come to the point of forgiving the deceased and moving on to rebuild their own lives.

Perhaps you are uncomfortable expressing your feelings in the presence of others. This is often true for men who are feeling sad or afraid. If it is true for you, you may find private expressions of feelings beneficial. Listen to a song, read a story or poem, go for a walk in a favorite place, or watch a movie on video tape that reminds you of your loved one. Allow yourself to cry if your tears flow; tell your loved one how much you miss her.

Many people direct the anger over their losses into building a network of rewarding friendships and activities. While these may not take the place of a cherished life partner, they do ease the loneliness.

5

ANXIETY AND GRIEF

Anxiety is a sense of uneasiness that resembles fear. It is a normal part of grief. "The distinction between anxiety and fear is essentially anxiety's absence of an object. Anxiety makes us feel nervous, distressed, uneasy, or unsafe, but we may not be able to identify a source directly; in contrast, we are usually afraid of something: pain, hunger, poverty, illness, humiliation, death," writes psychiatrist Stephen Shuchter in his book *Dimensions of Grief: Adjusting to the Death of a Spouse.* Since grief brings such a complex mixture of experiences and feelings, it is often difficult to tell the difference between anxiety and fear. The examples in this chapter will help you to recognize anxiety and to ease the problems it creates.

Anxiety often shows up as *physical distress.* It can make your heart race and can cause nausea, tightness in your throat or chest, sweating, difficulty in swallowing, headaches, and sleeplessness.

Anxiety attacks can cause such extreme panic or terror that many people who experience them wonder whether they are going crazy or whether they will ever be themselves again. Mundane tasks can become an ordeal. This was the case for one widow whose husband had always gone to the grocery store with her so they could "shop twice as fast." "The first grocery shopping trip after he died was a nightmare," she reported. "I was in line with a full basket of groceries. As I waited for my turn at the checkout, I went into a panic and thought I was going to faint." When she renewed her driver's license several months later, she had to wait in

15

line for an hour and a half. As the time wore on, she became nauseous. "It got worse and worse until I was so sick I thought I might have food poisoning or something. But, I knew that if I went home, I would just have to come another day, and my license was ready to expire. When I finally finished the test and went home, I was drained. I told my doctor about it, and he said that I might have had an anxiety attack. That's the first time I ever heard that this was normal after someone dies."

Anxiety can invade fears and worries that have some basis in reality and pump them up into full-fledged panic that paralyzes your judgment and your ability to carry out normal activities. For example, worrying about whether you can afford to continue your affluent style of living may be realistic. In the midst of an anxiety attack, though, you may panic over whether you can afford basic monthly phone service. An appropriate concern over the safety of your loved ones can escalate into frantic phone calls in the middle of the night to check whether they are safe.

Many people who otherwise cope successfully with their difficulties are thrown off kilter by anxiety or panic attacks after a major loss. If you have unresolved emotions from past crises or traumas in your life, you are more prone to suffer anxiety when a new load of pain is heaped on what is already there. Remember that people do get through this aspect of mourning. The following methods have helped others to manage and eventually overcome their anxiety.

The most often reported aid for anxiety is the *availability of someone who will listen sympathetically to your concerns*. You might arrange this by directly asking a friend, a pastor, a counselor, a family member, a doctor, or someone who has already gone through loss whether you may call them when you need a listening ear or reassurance. For instance, the widow who suffered the panic attack in the grocery checkout line asked a member of her support group for permission to call him in the middle of the night when she needed a few words of reassurance. "I never actually called, but knowing that I had that phone number was a comfort," she maintained.

One widower reported that he would plan one specific task for himself every day, whether it was completing an insurance form, packing one box of his wife's art supplies to give to a local school, or making himself a pot of soup that he could eat over the next few days. "That gave me something to show for my day," he said. "Otherwise I would wander around the house doing a little of this and a little of that. Then, at night, I would lie awake and worry about how I would ever get it all done."

Another antidote to anxiety is to sort through your worries and fears and separate the real dangers and legitimate worries from the anxiety. It is often most helpful to do this with the aid of a friend or someone who will gently nudge you back to reality when you stray from it. The following is a guide to help you through this process.

- Make a list of your fears and worries, whether they are large or small. For example: I'll spend the rest of my life alone. I can't carry on my life without her. I'll end up destitute.
- For each item on your list ask: How likely is that to happen? Give it a percentage estimate, ranging from zero to one hundred percent.
- Ask yourself: What power do I have to prevent this from happening to me?
- For the items over which you have some power, ask yourself: When will I start working on that?
- For the items over which you have little or no power,

ask yourself: How much longer, in my estimation, will I worry about it?

This exercise can help you sift out your genuine worries and fears from your anxieties and give you a sense of control in managing anxiety.

Remember that getting through this part of your grief is a step-by-step process, as is every other aspect of mourning. If your first attempt at managing your anxiety does not give you some relief, try other methods and then go back to the first one. You will gain more ease in managing this problem as your healing progresses.

6

LONELY GRIEF

Grieving is lonely under all circumstances. It is even more so when you do not have the full measure of understanding or acceptance from others that you wish you could count on. If your loss is not commonly viewed as one that merits deep mourning, you may not be able to find comfort from sources you would normally rely upon.

The death of a friend, for example, may bring more pain and longer mourning than you or others would expect. Your friend might have been closer to you than even your spouse. Perhaps you shared feelings and confidences or could rely on loving acceptance that you could not get elsewhere. This death is also a painful reminder of your own mortality. If your friend was your co-worker, you face the added loss of his warm presence amid the vagaries of the workday world. If your friend was an in-law or a member of your extended family, you may face the struggle of wanting to, or even being expected to, provide support for other mourners who had closer kinship ties to him than you did.

If your friendship was long-standing, you shared a rich history that cannot be replaced; you have lost someone who shared memories of your youth and of other persons known to the two of you. For example, one 73-year-old woman who had lost her lifelong friend described the painful jolt she felt every time she remembered that the phone would no longer ring at 10 in the morning. For decades that had marked the time to pour a quick cup of coffee and settle in for their daily visit.

If it is your sibling you mourn, even if he was 95 years

old, your loss can cause deep pain. As with the loss of other long-time relationships, this one reminds you of your own mortality. You have also lost a person with whom to share memories and to compare notes about your family history. If the relationship was characterized by conflict, the hope for forgiveness and acceptance is gone. If you and your sibling were close, that warmth and joy is now gone. Perhaps you overcame sibling rivalries and now grieve the loss of a person with whom you learned how to forge bonds that could withstand the stresses of human differences.

The death of a neighbor, even one who was not a close friend, can bring hardships which might not be recognized as grief. For example, if your next-door neighbor in your apartment building dies, you may be haunted by concern about what you could have done to help him in those last moments. If the neighbor lived in a house near yours, you might worry about who will move in next. The change might be yet another step in the transformation of your neighborhood from the one you have known for years. Next, you might wonder how much longer you will be able to, or wish to, live in your present home.

Losing a former spouse with whom you have a respectful relationship or even a deep friendship can bring grief that others might not understand. If your former spouse left a widow, your loneliness might be profound, yet she receives all the condolences.

Mourning the death of a grandchild can also be a lonely process. If he lived far away and your friends had little contact with him, you may find minimal support in your grief since your friends did not know him. Part of your pain is likely to be for the suffering of your own child who is facing this devastating loss. If you enjoyed a close relationship with your grandchild, your grief is compounded.

If you lose a pet, the effect can be "as profound and far-reaching as the loss of a human family member," writes psychologist Therese Rando in her book *Grieving: How To Go On Living When Someone You Love Dies*. With this death, perhaps you lost the one living being you could count on to love you unconditionally. Your pet might have been the one to greet you when you walked into an otherwise empty house or apartment. Yet the pain of such a loss is all too often met with misunderstanding or even criticism about why you are "taking it so hard."

If you lost a lover or a mate of the same sex, you may encounter people who do not recognize that the strength and tenderness of bonds in such a relationship can be as great as those of any other. When others do not know the nature of your relationship, you are likely to encounter their confusion as to how the death of your "friend" or "roommate" could cause such abject pain.

If you grieve the loss of a lover of the opposite sex to whom you are not married, your loneliness can be extreme. Should you choose to attend the funeral, you risk being the unwelcome outsider if your loved one had a spouse or family who knew, and disapproved of, the relationship. If the relationship was a secret, you might be an unknown party who receives inquisitive glances and little comfort. If you lived together or "dated" one another, the intensity of your sorrow might not be recognized because "you were, after all, not married."

If your loved one was devalued by society—for example, was mentally ill, died of AIDS, or was retarded, involved in criminal activity, or drug dependent—you face the cruel reality that you will be seen by some to have less need to mourn than if he had lived and died in the mainstream of society.

The circumstances of your loved one's death can affect the quality and amount of support available to you. For example, if your loved one committed suicide, there may be implied judgments that you should have done something to prevent it. Horror at the idea of taking one's own life can drive people away from any contact with, or reminders of, its occurrence. This situation can cause loneliness and isolation for you in addition to your grief. If the death was a homicide, the events surrounding the death may receive more attention than your needs as a griever.

Should you find yourself in circumstances like the ones described here, do not question whether you have a right to, or sufficient cause for, your pain. ". . . it is the nature and meaning of this particular loss to you that will determine whether mourning is necessary," Rando says. Recognize that you must *work through the grief* if you are to have any hope of healing the pain. Do not waste the precious energy that you need for mourning by seeking solace where there is none. If your current family or friends cannot provide you with what you need, find it elsewhere. There are support groups for various kinds of grief work. Rather than drifting into bitterness over the lack of support among those you would like to count on, allow them their opinions and seek a nurturing environment in which you can complete your grief.

7

GRIEVING THE TROUBLED RELATIONSHIP

Contrary to all logic, losing a troubled relationship often brings more painful and complicated grief than losing one marked by joy and fulfillment. The issues that remain in the wake of long-term disappointment are varied and difficult to face. It can take several years to resolve them.

First, the person you cared for is gone. Even if warm, spontaneous affection faded long before the death, you still had an investment in him or her. Any hopes or expectations you had for the relationship can never be fulfilled. This loss is part of the pain.

Your cherished dreams of warmth, closeness, harmony, acknowledgment, mutual support, cooperation, or joy in the relationship are dashed. Your hopes that somehow things will get better must be laid to rest. You must give up the search for the "secret" of what you could do to turn things around. With this death, a way of life ends—one built on habits of hoping, dreaming, and searching for the elusive and unattainable.

The pain of such a loss is often devastating because it is so intense and unexpected. One widow, for example, succumbed to serious depression for a year after her husband died. The long marriage had been wracked by his drinking and her resentment at being thrust into the role of primary breadwinner for the family. Her daughter said, "She's not the mother I've always known. I thought she would enjoy her freedom after

Dad died." Instead, the widow spoke of how she missed her husband. When her children reminded her of the discontent that had marked their marriage, she became indignant and told them that they should respect their father's memory. Counseling did not help. Eventually she required medical treatment for her depression.

There is a tangle of feelings to be faced if this grief is to be resolved. Many people feel relief that the stress of the relationship is now gone. Some welcome this relief; others feel guilty about it. You may feel guilt over past negative thoughts or behaviors toward the deceased. Perhaps, at times, you even wished to be delivered from the pain of the relationship through the death of the other person. Losing a troubled relationship can leave the survivor feeling angry at being cheated of realizing his dreams or receiving an adequate return for the time and effort invested in the relationship.

Some individuals do not work through the guilt, anger, and sadness of this grief and instead get bogged down in guilt over their part in the troubles of the relationship. Others remain angry with the deceased, blaming him or her for all the troubles. Some despair over ever achieving warm, cooperative, joyous relationships.

Another pitfall in resolving this grief is the tendency to focus only on the negative aspects of the deceased's life and character, failing to see her as a human being with the human combination of flaws and virtues. Idealizing the deceased—remembering only the positive qualities and losing sight of the person's full range of traits—is another difficulty. Both of these courses of action hide feelings that must be confronted if your grief is to be resolved.

For many survivors of troubled relationships, there is bitter regret that they spent their time in a situation

24

that held little promise of fulfillment. Coupled with this is the relief that the relationship is finally ended. Amid these mixed feelings, there is often the belief that things might have improved had there been more time. For example, one widow of a long, abusive marriage said, "I'm glad to have some peace from his temper. But still I wonder whether he would have acknowledged that I was important to him if he had just been able to come home from the hospital that last time."

If you are mourning a troubled relationship, you will make a crucial step toward healing when you confront your longstanding habit of living with pain and unhappiness. It is important to decide how you will replace this habit with others that can better serve your well-being. This requires that you recognize how you contributed to your own unhappiness in the relationship and learn how you can change those behaviors as you rebuild your life.

The following questions can assist you in this process.

- How did I use the relationship to perpetuate my habits of unhappiness?
- How do I continue to keep pain in my life by being guilty, resentful, or blaming?
- What is my fear of the future without the lost relationship?
- How do I use guilt, resentment, blame, or idealization to avoid taking care of my well-being?
- What do I get from holding on to habits or values that no longer serve my well-being?

By confronting your self-defeating patterns, you can protect yourself against drifting into them again.

Since this process is difficult and lengthy, it often helps to find a safe haven in which to do it. For example, look into grief support groups at churches, health centers, and hospices. Other alternatives may be joining an Al-Anon group or obtaining one-to-one counseling.

8

THE WIDOWER'S GRIEF

Women outlive men in three out of four marriages, so "men don't *expect* to be left alone," write Scott Campbell and Phyllis Silverman, Ph.D., in their book *Widower: When Men Are Left Alone.* Yet each year nearly a quarter of a million men in the United States become widowers.

If you are a widower, you are in the painful position of coping with one of the most stressful events in life, and you must do it in a world that is more responsive and accustomed to the concerns of women who lose their husbands. A poignant illustration of this is the man who lovingly prepared, and regularly updated for his wife, a guide to their financial affairs. He wrote instructions for her to follow when he died to make it easier for her to settle the estate. But, he was unprepared for the grief and loneliness he faced when, in a cruel turn of events, she died unexpectedly of a heart attack.

This man learned that he, like many men in our society, was seriously unequipped to handle mourning. Men customarily do not learn to experience or express the intense emotions of sorrow. At best, their repertoire consists of expressing anger. Other feelings get buried or mistaken for anger. Traditionally, women are more experienced in handling emotions and in tending to the matters of building and maintaining relationships. One widower observed, "Usually in a marriage, it is the wife who keeps the social life going. The wives call each other up, get together, do this, and do that," according

26

to Campbell and Silverman. Women typically arrange social events. They remind their men of birthdays and anniversaries. They frequently intervene in family conflicts to smooth ruffled feelings. Many men come to rely on their wives as their main source—and often single source—of emotional support. One widower expressed the vulnerability of this position: "I know the statistics. I know that women outlive men. That's what I always expected to have happen in my life. But . . . she died first. I didn't know what to do," Schiff writes in her book *Living Through Mourning: Finding Comfort and Hope When a Loved One Has Died.*

Widowers often work against serious handicaps as they strive toward a healthy resolution of their grief. When they are strangers in the realm of feelings, men are ill-equipped to cope with the normal sadness, fear, anger, and despair of mourning. To compound matters, many face abject loneliness at this time because their wives were their single emotionally intimate human contact.

Men are often unprepared for the basic tasks of managing laundry, meal preparation, shopping, and other household maintenance. When this is the case, they face yet another hurdle as they try to provide for their physical comforts in a time of need.

Some individuals assume that men do not suffer as intensely at the loss of a mate as women do. While it is unfortunate if the widower's friends or family hold this presumption, it is dangerous when the widower himself espouses this belief. This makes him vulnerable to thinking that he is somehow abnormal when the full force of his grief besieges him.

Under these circumstances, a man is susceptible to pushing aside his feelings or denying the stress of the grieving process. A significant number of men achieve this through remarriage. In their study of widowers,

Campbell and Silverman found that 52 percent of widowers remarry within the first 18 months, but that "over half of these early remarriages end in divorce or abandonment."

Attempts to escape from grief are dangerous to physical and mental well-being. The healthy alternative—to confront the pain and experience it fully—is the only way to get through it.

As a widower seeking to work through your grief successfully, it will be necessary to develop an acquaintance with this aspect of emotions. Many men find that they can do this best when they form connections with other men who have experienced and worked through grief in their own lives. It is "easier to learn from a peer than from an authority figure because a peer can talk your own language," according to Campbell and Silverman. Finding *acceptance and understanding for your feelings* from another human being is a vital step in your recovery.

Learn to take care of your daily needs for nutritious food, well-kept clothing, and a comfortable home environment. Politely yet firmly decline unwelcome offers of help in these aspects of your life. Discourage inappropriate "mothering" by female friends and your own family.

Instead of setting your sights on finding another relationship with a woman, work on rebuilding your life and developing your acquaintance with your feelings. As you develop the capacity to experience your feelings, you will be free to choose another mate when, and if, you believe it would enhance your life, and not because your survival depends on it.

9

GRIEVING THE DEATH OF A GROWN CHILD

"No one is ever truly prepared for death, his own or that of a friend, but when it is a child, the pain of death is so searing and unimaginable that no one is prepared to withstand its blow or accommodate his life to the loss," said Art Linkletter in *Grieving: How To Go On Living When Someone You Love Dies*. For most people, the loss of a child is the cruelest of all losses. It violates the order of life—the young are supposed to live on after the old, supposed to be there through their elders' decline and eventual death.

Part of the blow is the irretrievable loss of the care and effort you invested year after year. You had time to nurture and learn to love this person, to watch your child develop. Suddenly, the history you built and shared is snatched away.

The death of a grown child carries a brutal irony. You were spared from your nightmares of earlier years, of losing her to an accident or illness. Although she survived those dangers, you lost her anyway.

If she committed suicide, your pain is perhaps compounded by guilt because you did not, or could not, save her. If she was murdered or killed in an accident, you may feel rage, often fueled by the wish for revenge. You also must endure the pain that comes from your helplessness to protect your child from a tragedy.

The grief for this loss is complicated by many circumstances. If she was your only child, your role as a

29

parent is gone. Your direct descendent is gone as well. If she was one of several children, your unique relationship with her is not replaceable through your ties with other family members. Perhaps, you shared an interest in art or sports; perhaps the communication and companionship you had with this child was especially enjoyable. There are no substitutes.

In the event that you have grandchildren who still need care, perhaps you must decide whether or how much to help. Your decision can require adjustments of several kinds. If your health or financial means prevent you from pitching in as you would like, you may feel guilt or frustration. If you choose not to help for other reasons, you may have to cope with ambivalence about the soundness of your choice.

The death of your child may bring the end of regular contact with your grandchildren. If their other parent remarries, your relationship with him or her might dissolve, making it difficult or impossible for you to keep up your relationship with your grandchildren. Other sources of comfort, companionship, or support through in-laws, or even your child's friends, may also vanish in the aftermath of this death.

If your energy is depleted by health problems, you may be frustrated in your desire to channel your grief into volunteer service that could help to spare others a loss similar to yours. If your financial resources are limited as well, you may regret that you cannot channel your grief into helping others through monetary support.

You now face the realization that you can no longer count on this child to be present for you should you become dependent. If she was already helping to care for you, your loss and anxiety may be acute as you wonder who you can count on. If she provided you with emotional support and reassurance, you must now look ahead to a future without that comfort.

In this time of sorrow, you may find yourself in circumstances that deprive you of the full measure of support that you need. If your current friends did not know your child, they may not be as compassionate as you would wish. When a young or middle-aged adult dies, the condolences often go mainly to the surviving spouse and children. As an older parent, you may be seen as one who was not as intimately connected with the deceased as were those in her immediate circle, you may even be expected, by the family or by others, to provide emotional support to the spouse and children. Your response may range from indignation to despair and guilt as you find that your ability to give to others is at a lifetime low. Although you may ordinarily look to your spouse for support and comfort in times of hardship, you will probably find him or her far less responsive than usual this time since he or she is in pain as well.

Given all these difficulties and complications, it is small wonder that the loss of a child is recognized as the most excruciating pain known to humankind. "The death of your child exposes you to the most intense, complicated, and long-lasting grief known to humans. Unfortunately, most people fail to see its critical differences from other losses and don't understand that what is abnormal in those cases may be quite typical in the parental loss of a child," Rando writes.

It may well be in your best interest to seek assistance in the long journey toward recovery by joining a support group or obtaining individual counseling. "Although we are always accompanied by pain along the journey," writes Schiff in her book *Living Through Morning*, "the path we take and how we move along it can make all the difference in achieving a healthy recovery."

10

UNFINISHED BUSINESS

Whether death is sudden or follows a long illness, there is usually something left undone, unsaid, or unfulfilled. This is unfinished business—". . . those issues that were never addressed or settled in your relationship with the deceased," writes psychologist Therese Rando in *Grieving: How To Go On Living When Someone You Love Dies.*

Unfinished business is entangled with, and sometimes is the core of, the guilt, anger, and sadness of mourning. You will recognize your unfinished business as you recall the past and feel the pain of your "what ifs" and "I wishes" and "if onlys." Recognizing and finding suitable ways to resolve these issues are essential to completing your grief. Perhaps the following examples will help you to recognize some of your unfinished business.

Perhaps you are experiencing guilt or regret because you did not do more for the person before it was too late. If you did not get around to making an apology for hurtful behavior, or recognize signs of illness, or express your love more often, these issues need to be resolved.

You may be angry because you could not get something you desperately wanted from the deceased. Perhaps there was a shortage of affection or tenderness. Perhaps you wanted him to take more care in managing your joint finances so you would not be faced with a mess of loose ends to sort through. Maybe you longed for, and never received, acknowledgement of your achievements. Unfinished business often has to do with the lost expectations and hopes for your relationship.

Whether your hopes were for better times or for more of the good times you'd come to expect, there are no more tomorrows to count on.

The amount of unfinished business you have depends in part on whether and how you settled issues before the person died. Whether the backlog is great or small, it is possible to work through it, and doing so is vital to letting go of the past and rebuilding your future. The following methods have been used by people from many walks of life to deal with a variety of matters left unsettled by death.

One counselor working with a grief support group invites members at each meeting to tell their deceased one thing they wish they could have said. One man told his wife how he regretted having to admit her to a nursing home during the final stages of her struggle with Alzheimer's disease. The other members of the group gathered close to him as he wept and released some of his anguish over the losses he had endured through the last years of his marriage.

One widow wrote a letter of appreciation and regret to her husband who had died unexpectedly just a few months before he was to retire. She worked on the letter over a period of two weeks, since it was too painful to write in one sitting. The easiest part concerned her appreciation for the economic comfort and security he provided. She thanked him for being a faithful husband and a reliable father to their four children. However, she had great difficulty expressing her regrets: "He was a good man and I had so much to be thankful for that it was hard for me to write about my complaints. They seemed insignificant, but they bothered me just the same." She regretted that he had not been more demonstrative of his affection for her and their children. She always wished that he had joined with the family when they reminisced about the daughter who died in an auto accident at age 19. He always found something else to do instead. "And, I felt cheated that you died just before we retired because I looked forward to these years for you and me," she wrote. Later, she said, "I cried many times while I wrote this part of the letter, but I felt much better when I finished."

A 71-year-old woman decided to confront the unfinished business with her father who had been dead for many years. She arranged time for this one afternoon when her husband was away from home. She disconnected the phone to eliminate disturbances. Then, looking at his pictures in her album, she told her father of times when she longed for his support and understanding. She told him how she wanted hugs and reassurances rather than directives about how to solve her problems. She reminisced about the pleasant times they had enjoyed as a family. In closing, she told him that she loved him and appreciated the love she knew he had for her. Looking back on that afternoon, she recalled, "It was very difficult for me to do that, but after I did, I felt a peacefulness that lasted for several days. I began to notice, too, that I stopped being so hard on myself when I goofed up on little things."

As you resolve your unfinished business, you complete part of your history, filling in and smoothing over the gaps and the rough spots. This gives you a solid foundation on which to build your future. You will then be in a more favorable position to plan activities and relationships that fill your wants and needs.

11

WAYS TO SAY GOODBYE TO YOUR LOVED ONE

Saying goodbye to the deceased is your sign that you are ready to make the passage into a future where you can embrace new possibilities for your life, while honoring your past. Saying goodbye in a meaningful way frees you ". . . to remember and to love without pain, sorrow, or regret," says psychotherapist and social worker Judy Tatelbaum in her book *The Courage to Grieve*. Sometimes people resist saying goodbye because they are afraid it means putting a cherished person out of their lives. "It does not mean that you no longer love the deceased or that you will forget him," Rando writes in *Grieving*. Saying goodbye to your loved one after his death means only that you "let go of being connected to him as if he were still alive."

Your goodbye will be unique to you and your relationship with the deceased. It can be public or private, formal or informal, lavish or simple, dramatic or light-hearted, religious or secular, a one-time event or a process that continues over a period of time. The following examples illustrate a few possibilities for saying goodbye.

One widow invoked the Jewish custom of erecting a headstone on the grave one year after a person's death. "I worked on the design for weeks, remembering and crying all the while," she said. "When I knew it was complete, I felt peace and security for the first time since his illness. I invited our friends to the ceremony.

We shared our memories of him. That stone is an anchor for me. He always told me I was as sturdy ·as a rock, but I always thought my strength came from him. Since I survived his death, I learned that he was right. I know I'm as sturdy as a rock."

If you choose a religious ritual for your goodbye, you may select a special mass or memorial service on the anniversary of your loved one's death or birth. You might arrange to have a favorite prayer, scripture, song, sermon, poem, or reading in commemoration of the person. One woman held a birthday party on the second birthday after her lover died. Their friends cooked favorite foods. Before they ate, the group shared a goblet of wine. Each one took a sip and recalled a favorite memory of the deceased. The goblet made its way from hand to hand amid laughter and tears. After feasting and sharing more memories, the group watched a football game, an activity they had enjoyed together for many years.

A man whose two grown children had died in an auto accident used his artistic and architectural skills to design a stained glass window for his church. In a special ceremony, the congregation dedicated it to the memory of the young man and woman and to their surviving family members.

Some individuals say goodbye when they resume an activity or follow through on a plan they had shared with their loved one. For example, one woman completed her grief when she attended an opening night party at a favorite museum as she and her husband had done for years. A widower recalled, "A year after she died, Ruthie told me in a dream, 'Be sure and bring me a picture of a kangaroo, Freddie.' I knew she was telling me to pick myself up and start living again. So my son and I took the trip to Australia that Ruthie and

I were planning when she died. Since then, he and I are closer than we've ever been."

Your goodbye can be a personal or family ceremony. One widow and her three daughters shared farewell letters to their husband and father. As the moon rose, they released a balloon and said, "Go in peace and love." Many people plant trees or perennial plants in memory of their loved ones.

Tatelbaum explains the ritual of "finishing" as another way of saying goodbye. This process involves experiencing or expressing all the feelings connected with the relationship until the intensity dissipates. "The goal of finishing is to move feelings or experiences from foreground to background, to gain relief, and to attain some shift in perspective," she writes in *The Courage To Grieve*. You can "finish" through a conversation with the deceased, reading aloud a farewell letter or journal entries, or reminiscing. As you do this, allow yourself to express the mixture of positive and negative feelings that arise within you. When you "finish" in the presence of a support group or counselor, you will have the comfort of others who accept your full range of human reactions and encourage you to progress through them.

The timing of your goodbye depends on how much unfinished business you had with the deceased, how important the relationship was in your life, the nature of the death, and your coping resources. It can occur within months of the death or several years later. Usually when people allow themselves to feel the mixed emotions of grief, they are ready to say goodbye one to two years after the death. If you still have unfinished grief, it is never too late and always in your best interest to go ahead and feel the feelings. Then you can free your energies to live in the present and build your future.

12

SURVIVING THE
FIRST YEAR
OF MOURNING

"Sometimes there was a terrible black hole inside of me; other times I was inside of it," said one widow as she recalled her first year without her husband. As the first cycle of anniversaries, holidays, birthdays, and seasons approaches, you will experience changes for which even the most conscientious planning could not have prepared you.

Your feelings may run the gamut from sadness and anger to terror and despair. Your mental state can fluctuate between confusion and futile efforts to restore your life to order as soon as possible. You may fear that you are losing your sanity, your memory, your competence, and your health, all at a time when you need them most desperately.

Loss brings change that can shake the foundation of your life, so it is small wonder that many people experience the first year as being the worst time of their lives. There is a crushing amount of legal and administrative detail to handle, under even the best of circumstances. If the deceased shouldered responsibilities for major aspects of your life together, for example, finances, household management, legal matters, or social activities, you must learn to handle these as well as cope with the loss of the person. Many people focus on one aspect of the loss—the emotional pain, the financial concerns, legal matters, unfinished projects from their loved one's life, or the routines of their own daily lives—while allowing other aspects to go untended. Sometimes, there is no other practical way to survive; other times, it's an escape from a necessary part of mourning. Keep in mind that what you confront and handle, you can put to rest. One counselor said, "Grief is patient; whatever you leave undone just sits there waiting for you."

Here are some of the areas that will require your attention in the first year, and a few suggestions for handling them.

Emotional Matters

- Find friends, family members, a support group, or counselor who will listen, hold your hand, or visit regularly.
- Talk with your loved one, write a letter to her, keep a journal, or sleep on her side of the bed with a piece of her clothing next to you.
- Ask friends and family members for a hug when you see them.
- Give yourself time alone to reflect, to feel and release your sorrow.
- Kick a pillow, swing a tennis racquet, find a secluded spot to yell out your frustration.
- Talk with someone who has been through a devastating loss.
- Maintain your spiritual or religious activities.
- Allow yourself to cry.

Financial Matters

- Promptly submit insurance claims, enlisting help from friends or family members if you need it.
- Make a budget listing known expenses and sources of income before making large payments on outstanding bills.

- Review your health insurance. Get coverage if you don't have it.
- Take inventory of existing accounts, such as investment portfolios and other assets, so you can determine which to liquidate if necessary.
- Change joint accounts to your name.
- Apply for survivors benefits from your spouse's Social Security account, veterans' benefits, pensions, or annuities.

Legal Matters
- Get copies of the death certificate, which you will need for most transactions related to settling final details.
- Contact your attorney, or select one if necessary.
- Locate and file the will.

Daily Necessities
- Allow family and friends to help you by running errands or doing household chores during the first weeks.
- If you have a job or volunteer project go back to it after a leave of absence.
- Stay in touch with friends who accept your need to talk and express your feelings of grief.
- If it's at all practical, don't make major decisions about moving until you are further along in your journey toward recovery.

Physical Health
- Expect to be bone-tired and unable to sleep well.
- Exercise briskly at morning or mid-day to promote sleep and ward off depression.
- Eat nutritious foods whether you are eating more or less than usual.
- Maintain an adequate intake of vitamins and minerals.

- If you use sleep medications or alcohol, keep them to a minimum.

Mental Functioning
- Grief impairs your memory, concentration, judgment, organizational skills, decision making, and efficiency. Each day, make a list of small goals for your emotional well-being, financial/legal affairs, spiritual or religious well-being, physical health, and household maintenance.
- Keep in mind that most achievements during this period will take longer than you estimate.
- Make photocopies of documents you mail, and note phone conversations in a notebook. Write down phone numbers and account numbers as well as the names of people you speak with about your legal and financial matters. Use labeled manila folders or large envelopes for your notes and copies of forms.

Be patient and gentle with yourself as you mourn. Tend to the various aspects of your life at your own pace. This is your protection from getting mired in grief or escaping it through frenzied decisions you will later regret.

13

HOW LONG DOES GRIEF LAST?

Will time heal the pain of grief? Yes, if you make it your ally. The alliance will work if you allow yourself to feel your grief and let go of the past. Time will ease the sorrow of remembering and smooth the rough edges of your feelings.

Time will be your foe if you expect it to heal without your participation. Psychologist Rando likens it to the healing of a wound. "If your wound is cleaned and properly dressed, with time and treatment it will heal. However, if you ignore the wound . . . time will only mark the progress of festering infection," she writes in *Grieving*.

Assuming that you allow yourself to grieve, the duration of mourning will depend on the circumstances of the death, the nature of your relationship with the deceased, your personal coping resources, the quality of the support your receive in your time of need, and the impact of the death on the course of your life. If, for example, there was time to say goodbye to your loved one before his death, the period of mourning may be shorter than if death struck without warning. When the loss wreaks havoc in several aspects of your life, as when your spouse is both your business partner and best friend, mourning can be lengthy. Having your resources already stretched by other circumstances can prolong grief. One 76-year-old woman, for example, was struggling to adjust to the loss of sight in one eye after three unsuccessful surgeries. For the first time in her long marriage, she was physically dependent on her husband. When he died in his sleep unexpectedly, she was devastated by the pain of losing him, by an unplanned move to another state to be closer to her children, and by the loss of independent living. After 18 months of deep depression, she was finally able to grieve all her losses and start the journey toward recovery.

Adequate emotional support can hasten your recovery. People who have a limited supply of nurturance often have greater difficulty working through their grief than those who have abundant resources from which to draw. Many people find strength and support in their spiritual faith during times of sorrow. One woman explained, "I've maintained my faith throughout my life, so it is always there for me when I need it."

When the death frees you to pursue a postponed goal, the period of intense grief may be short. This was the case for one man who looked after, and eventually took complete care of, his sister through a long illness. At her death, his primary response was a quiet sense of anticipation and joy which he openly shared with his many friends. He had provided well for his sister and could at last realize his own dreams of extended travel. He had done most of the mourning for his sister and his delayed dreams prior to the death.

Even under the best of circumstances, mourning takes longer than is commonly assumed. While the intense pain often subsides in six months to a year, it can take longer than that to recover from the impact of the loss on the different areas of your life. Sometimes you will think you are finished with an especially painful aspect of mourning, only to experience it again. You might despair of ever getting through the pain, but you will.

Over time, your grief will fluctuate in intensity. Many people report that the first year is like a nightmare of remembering, longing, and confusion as they encounter the first holidays, anniversaries, birthdays, and changes of seasons without their loved one. While you may always find certain events and seasons to be bittersweet, you will know that you are recovering when the feelings lose their intensity. You will begin to notice that you have one or two "good days"; the good days will eventually stretch into good weeks.

Don't be afraid to acknowledge that there are some pieces of the past that you can quite happily leave behind. This occurs in the best of relationships, and acknowledging it is a sign of healing. For example, one widow recalled how she missed her husband on Sunday evenings when they used to host their monthly "Sunday Suppers." "For a long time, I stopped having them," she said. "Then I knew that I was doing better when I realized I could still do that without Ed." And, she smiled, "I could serve oyster stew, which I love but never made because he didn't like it."

14

HOW CAN MEDICATIONS HELP IN COPING WITH GRIEF?

There are two extreme positions regarding the use of medications as a tool to cope with grief. One is that the mourner can escape some of the wrenching pain of loss with the help of sedatives or tranquilizers. The other extreme position is that, under all circumstances, medications interfere with the healthy completion of mourning.

There is a middle ground in this dispute. This key discusses situations in which medications may be a useful tool in working through grief. After that discussion, we present some suggestions for working with your physician to determine when and how to use medications in this way.

It is not advisable to rely on medications to dull or block the emotional pain of grief. This practice only pushes aside feelings that will resurface until you face and work through them. On the other hand, medications can help you to muster your strength for the difficult process of grieving.

When a person dies after an illness, the survivors are often exhausted from the stress of the time spent at the bedside or from traveling to be with the dying person. As they start the difficult tasks of funeral preparations, they are already deprived of sleep. "Sleep deprivation can start a vicious circle of fatigue, anxiety, and hopelessness which prevents restful sleep," says psychiatrist Marita J. Keeling, M.D. This can lead to depression, which interferes with the completion of mourning. "The first choice in these cases is a mild sleep medication in small doses. Sometimes you can nip depression in the bud if you can get something to regulate your sleep," Keeling explains. She cautions that, because of the slower metabolism found in older people and the frequent presence of other medications, side effects must always be considered. "If it's at all possible, it is best to work with a physician who has had some experience in prescribing medications for older persons."

If you use sleep medications, take them intermittently. "Do not use them more than ten days at a time because after that you get hooked," Keeling says. For example, use them when you know you will need to be rested and are unlikely to fall asleep. "Take a small dose the night before the funeral, and perhaps the night after the funeral. Then go without it for a while," she suggests.

When signs of a major depression appear suddenly and last for two weeks or more, it is appropriate to consider medication. These signs include persistent pacing, agitation, restlessness, sighing, hand wringing, acting as if the deceased were still alive, sleep and appetite disturbances, loss of interest in normal activities, neglecting personal hygiene, or talk of suicide.

A mild sleep medication in small doses is the first choice of therapists for treating depression. If this does not relieve the symptoms, then antidepressants or antipsychotic medications may be in order. It is essential to watch for harmful side effects from such substances as well as for negative interactions with other prescription and over-the-counter medicines. In very rare instances, Keeling says, electroconvulsive (ECT) or shock therapy may be used to relieve the agony of severe depression. Today ECT is far more humane and effective than it was in the past, and, since it does not introduce substances into the bloodstream, it has less potential for negative drug interactions than medications.

Establish an "educated partnership" with your physician, Keeling suggests. This will set the stage for thoughtfully discussing your concerns about medications, whether you request them or whether the physician advises you to use them.

People are often concerned that using medication is an indication of weakness, mental illness, or emotional instability. They also fear getting hooked on habit-forming drugs. Many people know someone who has had unsatisfactory results from certain medications, and they are frightened of having similar experiences.

Air your concerns with your doctor. You might want to start out by asking, "May I take a few minutes to talk this over with you?" Ask questions about the potential side effects of a particular medication in light of the others you are already using. If you are uncomfortable about the medication prescribed, ask for more information about it. Ask what alternatives are available. If you have had a bad experience with a certain drug in the past, explain, "I've used this before and it knocks me out. Is there something else I could get that is milder?" If you want to take some time to gather more facts and think about using a medication, say, "May I call you again in a few days after I've looked into it and thought about it further?"

Information on medications is available through your pharmacist and local library. The *United States Pharmacopoeia with Dispensing Information* (USPDI), which contains facts in laypersons' terms about the various categories of drugs, is available at most pharmacies. The *Physician's Desk Reference* (PDR) contains detailed information in technical language and is updated annually. Ask your pharmacist to take a few minutes to explain the facts about a medication. Your local poison control center can also answer questions about prescription and over-the-counter medications.

"A physician usually feels more comfortable in working with a patient who will ask questions and share some responsibility for his or her care," Keeling says. Older adults often have doctors who are younger than themselves. When this is the case, an educated partnership with your doctor is particularly effective, suggests Keeling. You can establish mutual respect based on your doctor's technical knowledge and your experience with your body's unique responses to medical treatment.

15

USING PHYSICAL ACTIVITY AS A TOOL FOR COPING WITH GRIEF

Making your body an ally in managing the stress of grief can protect you from the many physical ravages grief can impose and ease your passage through the emotional pain. Think of physical activity as a powerful, versatile tool you can use for various purposes.

Activity can help you "to release your pent-up emotions," suggests psychologist Rando in her book. Sometimes it's difficult to talk about the anger, frustration, self-pity, guilt, anxiety, and depression that typically follow a major loss. The physical effects of such pain can be harmful unless it finds an acceptable outlet; vigorous physical activitiy can help in this regard.

Keep in mind that the definition of "vigorous physical activity" varies from person to person, depending on physical circumstances and personal preferences. This is discussed in more detail later in this Key.

Physical activity can bring you the gift of restful sleep by tiring your body in a healthy way. Plan your activities for several hours before bedtime. Go outdoors if possible unless temperatures, air pollution, or other conditions make it unsafe. To heighten the benefits of physical exertion, do relaxing, calming activities just before bedtime.

When you feel confused or anxious, the simple act of taking a slow, deep breath and exhaling slowly can help you to clear your mind for problem solving and to reground your thinking. Staying in bed beyond your normal sleeping hours won't help you escape your grief. The following activities can enliven your circulation, improve the oxygen supply to your brain, and help you get going. Take a slow, deep breath and expel it quickly and forcefully. Do this three or four times. Stretch your arms and legs gently, make the stretches larger as you repeat them three or four times. Then slowly sit up. Stretch your arms two or three times. Swing your legs over the side of the bed and slowly stand up.

Here are some examples of activities you can use to invigorate and calm your body and mind. Adapt them to your own circumstances or use them to spark your own ways of using your body as an ally in coping with grief.

Invigorating Activities
- Hitting your bed with a plastic baseball bat, a tennis racquet, or a pillow
- Bicycling
- Walking
- Swimming
- Dancing
- Shouting or screaming
- Calisthenics or an exercise class or a brisk workout using a cassette tape
- Climbing stairs
- Kneading bread
- Moving your arms as though directing an orchestra, marching, or dancing to a rousing piece of music
- Washing windows, cars, or walls
- Splitting wood
- Gardening

Calming Activities

- Breathe slowly and deeply.
- Close your eyes and cup your hands over them for 30 to 60 seconds.
- Slowly and gently rock your head from side to side with your eyes closed.
- Relax the muscles in your jaw and let your tongue relax on the floor of your mouth.
- Practice yoga.
- As you lie in bed or on the floor, systematically relax your muscles, starting from your feet and working up to your scalp.
- Take a warm bath or shower. One woman said "I've had some of my best inspirations from the Holy Spirit while relaxing in the bathtub."

As mentioned earlier, vigorous physical activity means different things to different people. Find something that fits your preferences and physical condition. If you're in a wheelchair or bedridden, for example, you might find that moving your arms for several minutes or even shouting and screaming are vigorous enough to help you release the tension of painful emotions.

Use physical activity as a way to be with others or to find solitude when you need it. For example, arrange time for a walk together when you visit a friend. On the other hand, taking a few minutes for a walk alone may provide the solitude you need in the middle of your first holiday gathering after your loved one's death.

16

USING RITUALS
TO EASE THE PAIN
OF GRIEF

"Rituals are ceremonies which mark the holy times of our lives," explains Clarissa Estes, Ph.D., a Jungian analyst and poet. She defines "holy" times as those deserving particuliar respect or reverence. Rituals at the time of death and throughout mourning afford you the opportunity to "interact intensely with the memory of your deceased loved one for a limited period of time in a healthy fashion," explains clinical psychologist Rando in her book. These ceremonies, whether formal or informal, are stepping-stones on the pathway toward healing and rebuilding your life.

Estes explains the significance of some of the traditional leavetaking rituals. Sitting with your loved one, for example, holding her hand, and stroking her forehead is a way to say goodbye and ease her passage into death. Choosing the garments in which to clothe her body for burial or cremation is a ritual through which you express caring and tenderness.

An open casket at the funeral provides an opportunity for another goodbye, another acknowledgment that your loved one is dead. Some people choose to place photographs from different periods of the deceased's life on the casket, using them to recall memories that the mourners can share with one another. The traditional walk to the gravesite symbolizes the part of your life's journey that you shared with the deceased. It's both a time for remembrance and for recognition that you will continue without her. In some cultures, each mourner throws a handful of dirt over the coffin when it is lowered into the ground to signify release of the dead back to the mother earth. "Black, the color of mourning," Estes explains, "actually symbolizes the fertile mud of the earth that awakens the new life in seeds committed to it through burial."

The customary gathering of friends and family after the burial is another important ritual, according to Estes. As people tell stories and laugh over humorous, heartwarming memories of the deceased, it "primes the pump" for more tears in a setting where it is acceptable for people to share freely the comfort of hugging and holding hands. "It's good for people to laugh until they cry, and to cry until they have no more tears left," Estes explains. "The tears are cleansing."

In the weeks and months following the death, rituals can help you to form a healthy attachment to your loved one's memory and to give lasting meaning to her life. Many people do this through dispersing their loved one's belongings. Some give the clothing or jewelry to family members and friends with a message about the significance of the pieces. One man, for example, gave his mother's sculpting tools to the community college where she taught classes. He arranged a time when the faculty from the art department could meet with him and share recollections of his mother and accept his gift as a tribute to her. For him, this event was a ritual, an exchange of gifts. The man acquired a deeper understanding of his mother's contributions as a teacher, and he put her tools in the hands of those who could keep them at work in his mother's memory.

Rituals can heal bitterness that must be put to rest. One family was devastated when their father shot himself after suffering a stroke. On the first anniversary of his death, the children planted a tree near the spot where he died to signify that he would always live in their memories.

Whether they are of your own design or follow traditional form, rituals are vital supports in moving through the mourning process. They help you to experience and resolve grief and act as milestones to mark the progress of your healing. Using rituals, you can honor and put your past to rest while deliberately choosing how to carry parts with you on your life's journey.

17

MANAGING YOUR LOVED ONE'S BELONGINGS

Find and follow your own timetable in dispersing your loved one's belongings. The following are some factors that will determine when you do this:

- Your preparedness for the death
- The age at which the person died
- Changes in your own living arrangements resulting from the death
- Your financial circumstances
- Your physical and emotional health
- Other demands on your time and energy
- The nature of your relationship
- Your geographic distance from the deceased and her property
- Volume and nature of the personal effects/property

Some mourners resolve their pain by going through the effects room by room, garment by garment. Many allot some time for the process each day or week. This can become a leavetaking ritual—touching the things your loved one used to shape her life and reinstating them to service in the lives of others. If disposing of the belongings in stages contributes to your healing, do it that way if it's at all possible.

One widow, for example, went through her husband's belongings during the year after his death. Her daughter helped when she came to visit. On those occasions the two women reminisced and shared their grief. Finally, there was only one desk drawer left. "I'm afraid of what

I might find there," the widow told her lay minister. As they talked, she realized she was putting off saying the final goodbye to her husband. She and the minister set a date on which they opened the drawer, sorted its contents, and visited the All Souls Walk at their church where the man's ashes rested. The woman understood that she did not have to put her husband out of her life when she bade him a last farewell.

Disposing of the personal effects can stretch out over decades. One woman lost an infant to Sudden Infant Death Syndrome (SIDS). Soon after that, her troubled marriage dissolved, and she immediately set about the job of raising her three other children. Twenty-four years later she asked her pastoral counselor to help her with a farewell ceremony for the baby. Only then did she put away the blanket in which the child had lain when she died.

Decline offers and pressure from others to dispose of your loved one's belongings quickly if this is possible. Wrenching yourself away from these connections before you are ready can result in bitter regrets later. Use statements like, "Thank you for your concern about me. I'm afraid of making decisions that I'll regret if I take this on too early. I could use your help in writing thank-you notes, though."

If you must disperse the personal effects before you are ready because of a change of living arrangements or other circumstances, take a few things with you—a pair of slippers, a shirt, or a wallet.

Disposing of your loved one's effects is not the same as stripping your life of all reminders of her. View it as a means of incorporating the past you shared into your future while clearing space to open a new chapter of your life. The rhythm you choose is up to you.

18

EFFECTS OF GRIEF ON FAMILY RELATIONSHIPS

There are two assumptions about grief and family relationships that can increase your distress and pain. One is that grief will draw a family closer together. Sometimes this happens, but reality may be quite the opposite. The second assumption is that family members can console one another.

Each member experiences and expresses grief at his own pace and in his unique way. For example, you might have suffered the wrenching pain of losing your brother as you nursed him through his long bout with Parkinson's disease; your middle-aged son, however, may weep bitterly throughout the funeral as he remembers childhood summers on his uncle's farm.

While individual members mourn the loss of a family member, the family unit must regroup and deal with the loss of one of its parts. Family units function harmoniously or otherwise because the members carry out certain responsibilities and roles. There are the obvious responsibilities like emptying the trash, maintaining the yard, cooking, and providing economic support. There are also less obvious roles or functions, such as peacemaker, troublemaker, communicator, or "sickly one." When a family loses a member's participation through illness or death, it "focuses on reestablishing balance in the system," writes Rando in *Grieving*. "Power, responsibilities, and roles will be reassigned as a result of the family's struggle to reestablish stability."

Each member of a family has his or her own relationship with the deceased, which affects the nature and intensity of grief. As one widower reflected on the effect of his wife's death on him and their six children, he said, "During the year after her death, I had time for long conversations with my oldest kids which I never had before. I learned that, in a sense, each of them had a different mother." Although some members of the family may have resolved conflicts with the deceased and enjoyed a fulfilling relationship, others may not have had much investment in the relationship, and still others may have backlogs of unfulfilled hopes or unresolved conflicts. The grief process for each of these can differ markedly, resulting in conflict or misunderstanding among the survivors if they are unaware of the complex nature of family relationships.

Members of the same family may also have remarkably different ways of expressing their grief. One person may have overt responses—crying or incessant talking about the deceased. Another may withdraw into silence. If family members pass judgments on each other's ways of grieving, it can cause distance among them.

The second assumption—that family members can console one another—is also fraught with danger. All too often family bonds cannot meet such expectations; for several reasons.

Mourning an important loss drains your emotional and physical strength. When family members suffer a common loss, they all feel depleted and may be of little consolation to one another.

When you grieve the loss of someone who was outside your family circle, it may not be possible to get the constant support that's necessary if you depend primarily on relatives who live far away from you.

Where family bonds are loose or conflicted, the stress of grief might be more than they can withstand. In such instances, a death may drive individuals further apart, especially if the deceased acted as peacemaker for the family.

Withstanding a common loss is particularly difficult for a couple when one or both of them depend on the relationship as their main anchor of nurturance and support at this difficult time in their lives. One counselor said that she urges couples to seek outside support or counseling when they lose a child: "That pain is almost too much for an individual to bear, and it's nearly impossible to comfort someone else when you are in that state."

Mourning can strengthen your relationships with family members under some circumstances:

- You learn more about one another by sharing your feelings, without attempting to extract more understanding and patience from your relative than she has to give you.
- You arrange to get adequate nurturance and comfort from various sources including friends, professional help, and self-help.
- You find ways to solve the problems that arise in your relationships with family members upon the death of a loved one. This can result in deeper warmth and enjoyment in certain relationships.

Grieving a death in the family may lead you to accept the fact that you cannot get the warmth and enjoyment you had hoped for from a particular relative. Such insight often improves a chronically troubled relationship because it frees you from the disappointment of seeking fulfillment where it isn't available. You can then use your energy to find it elsewhere.

You can use your journey through grief to grow out of a certain family role that no longer serves your well-being.

19

ARRANGING TO GET THE SUPPORT YOU NEED

You will need a variety of help to get through the mourning process. Some of it might be available within your circle of family, friends, and acquaintances; you may need to reach beyond that to get all the support you require.

First, there are the necessities of daily life, such as lawn care, thank-you notes, grocery shopping, house-cleaning, errands, car maintenance, and transportation for doctor's visits. Amid the confusion and fatigue of intense mourning, these can seem like unmanageable tasks.

These needs provide opportunities for others to bestow their kindness on you in truly helpful ways. When friends or relatives say, "If there is anything I can do, call me," they are usually sincere, yet hesitant to be pushy. Two or three suggestions from you can result in mutual benefits. Suggest, for example, that you need help writing or addressing thank-you notes or mowing the lawn, or that you could use a ride to the doctor's office on Tuesday morning. Accepting the help you need can deepen the bonds of friendship and enrich both of you.

Since the mixture of needs you have at this time of your life cannot possibly be fulfilled by one source, be prepared to look to multiple individuals and resources. Some of your friends and family will be better at helping with household tasks or with paper work, while others will be adept at giving emotional support. When the people who are concerned about you and love you can ease your pain through their generosity, it is a gift to them and to you.

Many people express their concern for a bereaved person through comments that unwittingly offend rather than comfort, such as, "He has moved on to a better life now," "Be thankful for all the happy years you had," or "There, now, she wouldn't want you to be so unhappy." While remarks like this might be true, they can be cold comfort when you are mired in loneliness and despair. If you wish to acknowledge the concern that lies beneath such a comment, you could respond with, "Thank you for your concern." Or you might simply touch their hand or accept a hug. This allows you to soak in the kindness that is available to you.

Remember that you don't have to remain deprived if your present circle of support is limited or if it dissipates before your need is satisfied. One bereavement counselor commented that grieving persons often have a flurry of attention and support for the first couple of months after the death. Friends and family call, visit, and inquire about your well-being. In a few months, they resume their lives and assume that you will, or should, do likewise. That is often the time when the full impact of the loss is just setting in. You'll need someone who understands how important it is for you to talk about the deceased, to tell the same stories time and time again and to vent your frustration about the unfairness of your plight. You will need someone to reassure you that you are a good person and that many people experience guilt, hatred, regret, or vengefulness such as you might during this difficult time. You will need people to listen as you figure out how to solve your problems, who will give suggestions only when you ask for them, and who can understand that you might choose not to follow their advice. Finally, you will need someone to gently remind you that your pain will diminish in time without pushing you to cover up your pain in a pretense that you are recovering on schedule.

This person will not be afraid if you weep or rage in anguish, nor will she tell you that you "shouldn't feel that way." She will accept that you must often contradict yourself, doubt yourself, and repeat yourself as you muddle through this troubled, dark period. She will understand that, as you mourn this loss, you may experience a surge of grief over past losses, especially those you had not fully mourned.

This person must have the emotional resources to comfort and nurture you, as well as the understanding that you cannot reciprocate at this time. Sometimes it's easier to express your feelings to someone who is fairly detached, rather than a close friend or relative, but who still can offer acceptance and caring.

Perhaps you are fortunate enough to have a friend, relative, counselor, or support group who can help you in this way. If you want this support from a friend or family member, ask for their consent first, because helping someone through grief consumes large amounts of energy, especially when there are personal ties involved. Explain what kind of support you want—for example, phone visits when you feel lonely, lunch dates once a week, hikes together, or help in sorting through the personal effects.

Whether you are newly bereaved or carry unresolved grief from a past loss, it's time to help yourself by getting the support you need to complete your mourning.

20

HANDLING UNWANTED HELP

Don't be surprised when people try to help you in ways that appear more bothersome or hurtful than comforting. Our culture has a dim understanding of grief and an irrational fear of death, so it is no surprise that many people do not know how to help and comfort the grieving. Differences in people's needs present a further complication; what is helpful to one person might be intrusive to you.

Here are some ways to turn unwanted help into genuine support and to protect yourself from intrusions.

- When people pressure you to make decisions before you are ready, say, "Thank you for your concern. I know that I must make those decisions eventually, but I'm not myself at this stage. I plan to wait until I trust myself to do something I won't regret later."

- Tell your friends and family how they can help you the most. For example, you might find that phone calls are awkward in the early months because you end up in tears. You can tell your friends, "I find that notes or postcards with things you remember about Ann are such a comfort to me. I read them over and over again."

- If friends or family press you with suggestions or advice, invoke a light touch and outside backup that conveys your firm position: "My counselor holds me strictly accountable every time I say yes when I want to say no!" or, "My accountant told me not to even talk about it for another three months."

- When a dear friend or relative besieges you with well-intentioned efforts to help, offer her an opportunity to learn more about mourning and the kinds of help people need to get through it. For example, you might say, "Grace, I didn't understand how complicated grief is until a member of my support group gave me this little book. It helped me see what it's going to take to get myself through this. I wanted to share it with you because you've been so concerned about me and I treasure our friendship."

- Be assertive in handling calls from would-be financial advisors, insurance representatives, and others who sell their services. Stick to your point and don't be pressured into scheduling "introductory visits" concerning services you don't want. Say, "Thank you. I am not interested." If the caller persists, "But Mrs. Jones, have you considered . . ." simply repeat your point more firmly: "Thank you. I am not interested." And hang up the phone.

- Limit the time you spend with persons with whom you want to be in touch but who cannot offer the support you need during the intense stage of grief. Arrange to meet them for lunch on a day that you have a doctor's visit, a counseling session, or a massage scheduled a couple of hours later. By doing this, you can control the amount of time you spend at the same time you're nurturing yourself.

- Have a "home base" of support that you can count on for acceptance, reassurance, a sense of humor, and patience, as well as gentle confrontation when you sabotage your progress toward healing. Home base might be one or several of the following: close friends, family members, grief support groups, pastors or rabbis, counselors or therapists. Using this support fully enables you to keep your dignity and self-esteem as you deal with the unwanted help.

21

FINDING AND USING GRIEF SUPPORT GROUPS

Grief support groups are regular gatherings of individuals who help each other through the mourning process. An important benefit of group membership is the opportunity for contact with others who are at various stages of mourning; those in the group who are beyond the early stages of mourning guide and encourage the newly bereaved. Seeing others who have regained fulfillment and joy in their lives can bring hope at a time when pain seems overwhelming and unending. Many group members report that a vital part of their own healing consists of helping other mourners understand grief, accept loss, and rebuild their lives.

Some support groups are led by professionally trained facilitators; others are run by group members who occasionally invite resource persons from the community to give presentations. Healing occurs through mutual sharing of experiences, through being understood by others who have had similar pain, through the nurturing and acceptance among group members, and through the exchange of information about coping with loss.

Support groups are often organized for survivors of different types of loss. For example, there are groups for parents who have lost children and other groups for those whose loved ones have died from suicide or homicide, groups for those who have lost mates of the same sex, groups for those whose loved ones have died of lingering illnesses, and still others for bereaved pet owners. Some losses are best mourned in special support groups, where members can find the understanding, compassion, and acceptance for their grief that might not be available from other sources. Cases involving suicide, AIDS, or homicide are examples. Others include the loss of a same-sex mate, a close friend, a lover, or a pet. Here, compassion and understanding are available as well as the sustained support you'll need long after others think you should be over your loss.

When is it appropriate to join a support group? The most reliable rule of thumb is to *act on your own needs and circumstances.* If you don't have a nearby circle of supportive friends and relatives, a support group can provide immediate assistance and access to people who may later become friends.

Support groups can be helpful several weeks or even months after the death of your loved one. Sometimes it takes that long to move from the initial shock into the next phase of grief. By this time your friends and relatives may assume that you have recovered and they return to life as usual, while your need for support is greater than ever. When Dorie Furman found herself in this situation five months after her husband's unexpected death, she joined a chapter of Widowed Persons Service (WPS). "My family thought it was time for me to shape up, but I was still devastated," she said.

If you are fortunate enough to receive understanding and compassion from your friends and family but think a support group could offer additional help, that's reason enough to join one. Perhaps you want outside resources to keep from overburdening your family and friends. Remember that through your presence in a group, you become a resource to others as well.

It's never too late—if you suffered a loss a year ago, or even more, and still can't rebuild your life as you would like, a support group may help.

Here are a few guidelines for determining whether a particular group is suitable for you:

- When you make your first inquiry, note whether the contact person is helpful and takes the time to answer your questions.
- If you're uncomfortable coming to a meeting alone, ask whether you can meet another member of the group ahead of time and attend the first meeting with her.
- Visit once. Listen and observe whether you have enough in common with the members to fit in with the group.
- Consider whether you feel accepted by, and comfortable with, the members and leader.

The length of time you spend in a support group depends on your needs. Some people stay through the acute stages of loss, for example, six weeks to three months. Some stay longer. They complete their own healing by helping others. Furman, for example, took a volunteer training class and then became president of her WPS chapter four years after her husband's death. "There's such a need for people who understand what the pain is like. I wanted to help others in any way I could," she says.

The number of support groups is growing. In many locations, you can choose from several alternatives. Start your search by checking with your own church or others in your community. Hospitals and hospices often sponsor groups or have social workers who can help you locate one. Older adults' (senior citizens') community centers and health centers often have support groups. You can also check with your friends and relatives, your doctor, community social service agencies, and community mental health centers.

If there are no groups in your area, consider starting one. It can be an important way to help yourself through the grieving process. Many groups owe their existence to persons who used their grief to help others. Starting

Mothers Against Drunk Driving (MADD), for example, was Candy Lightner's response to the death of her daughter in an accident caused by a drunk driver. MADD has been instrumental in the enactment of drunk driving laws and victims' rights programs and in the development of extensive public education about the problems of drunk driving.

To locate support groups in your area, contact WPS through the American Association of Retired Persons (AARP), 1909 K Street, NW, Washington, D.C. 20049; (202) 872-4700, or the Self-Help Clearinghouse, St. Clares-Riverside Medical Center, Pocono Road, Denville, N.J. 07834; (201) 625-9565.

Support groups cannot substitute for professional counseling when you need it. The next two Keys provide information on this topic.

22

WHEN IS PROFESSIONAL HELP USEFUL?

Some people use psychological counseling or therapy much as they use the services of their family doctor to resolve problems and maintain their health. One woman commented, "I can't imagine *not* getting counseling for grief." If you're not accustomed to using professional help, you might wish to consider it as a tool to help yourself at this milestone in your life.

In any of the following circumstances, professional help could be invaluable:

- You cannot find the nurturing and acceptance you need within your present circle of friends or family, particularly after the first weeks of mourning.
- You wonder whether your grieving behaviors are "normal."
- Your loss has triggered other drastic changes in your life, for example, living arrangements, shortage of money, or a need for assistance with daily activities due to your physical problems.
- You wish you had more effective coping skills.
- Family conflicts are compounding your emotional pain.
- You want to learn ways to deal with the well-meaning attempts of others to advise or help you.
- You want to learn how to build a circle of supportive relationships.

In the following instances, professional help is *strongly* advised:

- You have regular outbursts of rage or aggressive behavior.
- You experience loss of appetite, severe insomnia, confusion, hallucinations, constant pacing or hand-wringing, inability to get out of bed in the mornings, or loss of interest in your personal hygiene for more than two weeks.
- Your changes in eating habits and weight persist for more than a year.
- You have a history of bipolar illness, depression, alcoholism, heavy use of legal or illegal drugs, or suicidal behaviors.
- You have persistent thoughts of suicide.
- You have started to engage in reckless driving, excessive drinking or smoking, use of medications or illegal drugs, gambling, or promiscuous or unsafe sexual activity.
- Your grief, preoccupation with the deceased, guilt, or hostility have not let up after two to three years.
- Several people have suggested that you seek professional assistance, particularly if they themselves are professionals—for example, your minister, rabbi, physician, dentist, or attorney.
- You regularly find yourself in situations that threaten your safety, personal comfort, or peace of mind.
- You still find your life devoid of pleasure one to three years after the loss.

In the end, you must decide whether to enlist professional help as a tool in resolving your grief. Even if you think you don't actually need it, you might do yourself a service to check into it. At the same time, don't do it just to please or frustrate someone else; you'll waste your effort and money. One requirement for successful counseling or therapy is your *participation* in making the personal changes necessary to achieve a better life.

23

FINDING PROFESSIONAL HELP FOR COPING WITH GRIEF

Be a discerning, prudent consumer when you seek professional help. First, know all of the options that are available. Think about which ones best suit your circumstances and personality.

If you decide on *individual counseling* or *therapy,* you can choose from a variety of professionals, including social workers, psychotherapists (qualified by various educational backgrounds), psychiatrists (medical doctors with M.D. degrees), psychologists (who usually have Ph.D.s in psychology), pastoral counselors, and ministers or rabbis. Your sessions will be regularly scheduled, usually occurring two to four times a month. Each one will last 40 to 50 minutes.

Group counseling or *therapy* combines the help of a trained counselor and the support of others who are dealing with grief or other personal matters.

Some people prefer group settings because they offer opportunities to learn from, and exchange support with, individuals who are pursuing positive life styles. Strong friendships often develop among group members. For others, the need for a caring, supportive relationship with one person is best fulfilled in individual counseling.

Peer counseling is another option for assistance in resolving your grief. Here you will find help through a one-on-one relationship with a person who has had experiences similar to yours. Peer counseling resembles a close friendship. The counselor, usually a volunteer, is trained to listen and to be helpful, not bossy. She will guide you to other sources of help if that seems necessary.

Sometimes the most difficult problems to resolve after a death are the conflicts that arise among the survivors. If that is your case, *mediation* might be your best option. In mediation, a trained, impartial third party helps disputants negotiate and reach their own solutions without telling you what to do or judging whether you are right or wrong. Mediation can help settle persistent conflicts or disputes with others for whom you may or may not feel great fondness. These people may include tenants, landlords, business partners, neighbors, or even relatives. Families sometimes benefit from mediated settlements of conflicts over caregiving, end-of-life decisions, or estates.

The size of your community will determine how many resources are available. You can find leads through:
- Word-of-mouth from friends or relatives
- Minister or rabbi
- Senior centers or clinics
- Family physician
- Community centers
- Community calendars in your local newspapers
- Mediation centers
- Funeral directors
- Community mental health centers
- Hospital departments of social services
- Hospices
- Local department of social services
- Local mental health association
- Telephone book listings for mediation services, mental health services, psychiatrists, psychologists, psychotherapists, senior citizens' services, social service organizations, and social workers
- Widowed Persons Service—contact either your local

chapter or the national headquarters, located at American Association of Retired Persons (AARP), 1919 K Street, NW, Washington, D.C. 20049; (202) 872-4700

- Senior Companion Program—call your local chapter or the national headquarters located at ACTION, 1100 Vermont Avenue, NW, Washington, D.C. 20525; (202) 634-9349

As you check out the various resources, be as choosy as you would be if you were searching for any other important product or service. Leave no question unasked. Ask about fees and ask for references. Ask the therapist or counselor how much experience she has and what approach she uses in helping people through grief. Ask whether she accepts clients who want short-term therapy. Ask about insurance coverage for her services and when payment is expected. Note that although there is usually no fee for peer counseling, sponsoring organizations sometimes request donations to help with the cost of training the volunteer counselors.

After the first contact with your potential counselor, ask yourself, "Do I feel respected and cared for here?"

As psychotherapist Yancey Stockwell says, "All the training and expertise in the world is worth nothing to you if you don't feel respected and cared for by your counselor."

Take stock after using the service for a while. Ask yourself, "Am I learning some useful ways of managing or solving my problems? Is there hope and comfort here for my aching heart?" If you can answer yes to both questions, then you've found the professional help you need.

24

WHAT NEEDS IMMEDIATE ATTENTION?

A barrage of paperwork starts hours after a death and continues for several months. It will be somewhat more manageable if you confront the urgent details right away and get to the others as you have time. Depending on your relationship to the deceased, you will need some or all of the following documents to handle the immediate details:

- Copies of birth certificates: The deceased's, your own, any minor children and the spouse of the deceased
- The marriage license
- The military discharge certificate if the deceased was a veteran
- The will
- Life insurance policy
- Records of prefinanced burial arrangements
- Death certificate (Ask the funeral director to get them for you. You might need as many as 12 originals for insurance claims and survivors' benefits; photocopies are not acceptable in most cases.)

Put the following identification numbers on a card and carry them in your wallet:

- Social Security numbers of the deceased, any minor children and the spouse of the deceased, your own
- Bank account numbers
- Credit card account numbers
- Credit card insurance policy numbers if such insurance was in effect
- Health and life insurance policy numbers

- Mortgage or loan insurance policy numbers
- The phone number where you can be reached

Tend to the following matters personally, or ask someone to help you with them:

- Notify relatives, friends, the deceased's church, employer, groups or organizations where he did volunteer service.
- Determine the location and conditions under which the safe deposit box may be opened.
- Notify the deceased's attorney, accountant, and/or financial advisor.
- Set up a new bank account to handle funds from insurance policies and survivors' benefits.
- Put all incoming mail in one place even if you use just a simple container like a shopping bag or laundry basket.
- Use a notebook to jot the times, dates, names, and topics of phone conversations, whether they pertain to business, funeral arrangements, or condolences.
- Check on the existence of a letter or instructions from the deceased about his desires for funeral services, burial, or cremation.
- If the deceased was a veteran, call your local Veterans Administration about burial benefits and possible interment in a national cemetery. Find the number in the U.S. Government section of the telephone directory.
- In the absence of existing funeral plans, make arrangements based on the resources available. Resist the pressure to make expensive arrangements that could jeopardize your financial future. Wait a few months to select a headstone or resting place for the ashes.
- Change joint bank accounts into your name.
- If you were covered by the deceased's health insur-

ance, notify the agent or insurance company of the death and make sure you're still covered. If you are handling final details for a friend or relative, make sure that they and any dependents are covered by the deceased's policy.

- Notify the deceased's life insurance agent or company. If the company offers the proceeds in monthly payments rather than a lump sum, be aware that you have a choice. Request a lump sum if you want it. If you urgently need cash to cover immediate expenses, some life insurance companies will advance up to ten percent of the policy's proceeds to the beneficiary. Check with the company or agent about this possibility

- Notify creditors of the death and explain that there might be a delay in payments on outstanding bills.

- Make photocopies of everything you mail or hand over to others.

- Don't pay bills until you have determined what assets are available.

- Don't accept any COD packages addressed to the deceased. Refuse demands for repayment of loans said to be owed by the deceased. Don't pay "overdue premiums" on insurance policies said to be owned by the deceased. Be sure that communications from the Veterans Administration (VA) are bona fide. Any "VA" funeral services you may be offered that are not listed in your VA benefits brochures are probably shams. If you're in doubt, call the VA for verification.

- Put a pad of paper and pencil in every room so you can make notes of things as they occur to you.

25

FILING INSURANCE CLAIMS

"Insurance companies are wonderful about paying off if you ask them, but they don't come looking for you," says one financial planner. You may be entitled to more than you expect in the form of insurance proceeds. This money may ease the worry of looming debts from your loved one's final illness, the funeral, outstanding loans, or daily living expenses. This Key explains how to find policies the deceased may have forgotten and provides general tips to use when filing all claims.

Medical or Health Insurance

In addition to primary medical insurance, many people purchase *hospital indemnity plans*. These pay a specified dollar amount per day for hospital confinement. The conditions are stated on the policy, including the time limit for collection of benefits. If you cannot locate the policy itself, look for cancelled checks or go through the check registers for clues to the name of the company or a policy number. Even if the collection period has expired, it may still be possible to receive full or partial benefits. You have nothing to lose by filing, the worst that can happen is that the company will deny your claim.

If the deceased had Medicare and supplemental insurance to cover what Medicare excludes, submit all the claims to both. Then write a letter to each person and organization that sends a bill, including the deceased's Medicare number, the supplemental insurance policy number, and a copy of the death certificate. Ask the creditors to accept "Medicare assignment" as payment in full. If they accept assignment, you or the estate will save out-of-pocket expenses.

If the deceased had group medical insurance with a company that went bankrupt or is in the process, you may be able to collect partial payment on the outstanding bills as one of the company's creditors. Ask for assistance from the U.S. Department of Labor's (DOL) regional Pension and Welfare Benefits Administration office. Call your local DOL office for contact information.

Life Insurance

The deceased may have had several life insurance policies. The primary one is probably among the important papers; others may be in drawers or boxes long since forgotten. If you find evidence that there was insurance, but cannot locate the actual policy, contact the insurance company for a lost policy form.

Major credit card companies often provide death benefits for card holders who die in airplanes, cars, or trains if they charged part of their travel expenses to the card. Credit unions sometimes pay death benefits for savings account holders. If the deceased was a dues-paying member of a professional society or a labor or fraternal organization, call to inquire whether he had a group life insurance policy.

Credit Card and Loan Insurance

The deceased may also have had coverage for credit card balances and bank loans. If you don't find evidence of such coverage among the deceased's personal effects, call the customer service phone number listed on the credit card or the monthly statement to ask if such coverage was in effect. For a bank loan, call the lending institution.

Annuities
- If you find cancelled checks, account statements, or receipts indicating the existence of an annuity but can't find the policy, contact the company and request a lost claim form.

Tips for Making Insurance Claims
- Ideally, you should file claims within 90 days of the death, but it's never too late.
- Fill out each form completely and correctly to avoid delays.
- For life insurance claims, write a simple letter including the deceased's name, date of death, and policy number. Enclose a copy of the death certificate and the policy, if you have it. State that you wish to receive the payment as soon as possible. If the death was due to natural causes, expect a check within a month. Payment for an accidental death can take longer if the insurance company conducts an investigation.
- To locate an insurance company not listed in the telephone directory, call your state's insurance commissioner for an address.
- When filing health insurance claims, send a copy of the statement of services received rather than a copy of the bill.
- If you are overwhelmed with paperwork or can't bring yourself to search through things for important documents, there are a number of ways to make the task easier. Ask a friend or family member to help you by spending a few evenings organizing the paperwork, filling out forms, or making photocopies before mailing out the claims. You can ask your local American Association of Retired Persons (AARP) chapter or

your senior citizens' center how you can get help with your insurance forms. Ask your trust officer, financial advisor, insurance agent, or accountant for assistance. (Be sure to inquire about their fees first.) Hire a bookkeeper or an insurance claims specialist to help you. Some individuals charge hourly fees for this service; others agree to receive a percentage of each claim they collect as their compensation.

- Heed the advice of one insurance broker: "When in doubt, submit the claim. Even if a medical policy excludes certain illnesses, it might pay for procedures connected with it. The most they can do is deny the claim, and they will tell you the grounds on which they deny it.

- "If a form comes back to you with the word 'Denied,' read it; don't throw it away. It might just be saying that *part* of your claim is denied, or that they need more information before they can process it."

26

HANDLING SOCIAL SECURITY BENEFITS

Contact the Social Security office immediately after the death of your spouse to minimize any delay in receiving survivor's benefits. You won't get them unless you apply. Find the phone number for your local office in the telephone directory listing under U.S. Government, Social Security Administration (SSA).

As a widow or widower you may be eligible for:

- A lump sum death payment of $255 (you must apply for this within two years after the death).
- Monthly payments based on your spouse's earnings and Social Security credits. The amount will depend on your age. You are allowed to collect either your spouse's benefits or your own. Most people opt for the larger amount. The SSA can help you figure which amount will be larger.
- Disability benefits if you are age 50 or over and disabled.

If you are divorced from the deceased but the marriage lasted at least ten years, you may be entitled to monthly payments even if you are remarried. The amount of the payments will depend on your age.

If you lost a mate of the opposite sex and live in a state that recognizes common-law marriages, you may be eligible for survivor's benefits if you can prove to the SSA's satisfaction that you had such a relationship. The SSA does not at this time recognize survivors of same-sex relationships as eligible for survivor's benefits.

In recent years the SSA has streamlined its procedures with the help of computer technology. The result is greater convenience for you as a beneficiary, but you must protect your interest by reviewing all paperwork details. Benefit payments usually start within a few weeks.

You can apply for benefits by phone in most cases. An SSA representative will explain the procedures and schedule a telephone appointment. You will probably need the following documents:
- Social Security numbers for yourself and the deceased
- The death certificate
- Proof of your age
- Your marriage certificate
- The divorce decree if applicable
- The most recent W-2 forms or, for self-employed persons, the federal tax return
- Your checkbook, savings account passbook, or papers showing your name and account number as proof that you do business with your financial institution (if you plan to have the checks deposited directly into your account)

If you have a low income or are blind or disabled and have few assets, you may qualify for Supplemental Security Income (SSI). This will provide you with a minimum monthly income as well as social services and, in most states, valuable health care coverage under Medicaid. The SSA representative will give you details.

To protect yourself from errors, both your own and those made by the SSA, keep notes of each conversation, including the representative's name, what he or she promised to do, the estimated time the action will take, and how you are expected to follow up on the matter. Make photocopies of all paperwork before sending it out; copy machines are available at your bank, grocery store, library, post office, pharmacy, or stationery store.

If you must go to the Social Security office for a personal appointment, ask a friend or family member to go with you. It's often easier for someone who is more detached to remember details and ask questions without getting emotionally involved.

The SSA offers the following tips to make your application as smooth as possible:

• Don't wait to apply because you are missing some of the necessary documents. Representatives can start the process and suggest other proofs you can substitute.

• A word about timing: "Because most calls from current beneficiaries occur the first week of the month, and on Mondays and Tuesdays of other weeks, your call will be handled more promptly if you call at other times in the month," according to the booklet "*Survivors*" published by the Social Security Administration. Early morning and late afternoon are the best times to call. Of course, if your business is urgent, call immediately.

The SSA is committed to providing the best service possible. If you don't receive a courteous or prompt response in spite of repeated attempts, ask to speak to the manager of the office with which you have been dealing. This is where your careful notes about your transactions will be useful. Once in a while, it's necessary to go even further than the manager. In that case, you can explain your problem to the staff at your Congressional representative's office. If you keep notes of your conversations and are persistent, you're likely to get results.

27

COLLECTING PENSION BENEFITS

As a survivor, you must claim your pension benefits; otherwise, you may not get them. You may be entitled to survivor's benefits from any of the following sources:
- private employers
- the Veterans Administration (if your spouse served in the military)
- an Individual Retirement Account (IRA)
- a Keogh plan
- a deferred compensation plan
- annuities

Here are some guidelines for what you might expect and tips of how to claim your benefit.

Private Employers

If your spouse was employed when he died, contact the employer within a few weeks after the death. Inquire about survivor's benefits from your spouse's pension plan. Collect the final paycheck, any unpaid bonuses or commissions, and money from unused sick leave or vacation if it's available according to company policy. If you have questions, ask for a copy of the employee handbook or a written statement regarding the company's policies on survivor's benefits.

If the employer has gone bankrupt or is in the process of doing so, the solvency of the pension plan should not be affected. Federal law requires that companies keep their pension funds separate from their operating funds, so you should be able to collect your survivor's benefits even under such circumstances. The U.S. Department of Labor (DOL) suggests that survivors deal in writing with the "plan administrator," which can be either an individual or an organization. Find out who to contact by checking the employee handbook or asking the company's employee benefits department. "Get everything in writing and make copies of all correspondence," suggests a DOL representative.

Make a list of all your spouse's employers and contact each one; sometimes there are pension funds waiting to be claimed from jobs held as far back as 30 years ago. Look through all the paperwork for anything that looks like an official document or has notes of account numbers or payments. These can be clues to "stashes" that have accumulated interest over the years. One financial planner said that a few hours of effort going through old papers, produced an $89 monthly benefit for a widow with limited means and a $25,000 lump sum payment for another family.

If you don't know how to track down former employers or how to interpret official-looking documents, ask you accountant, trust officer, attorney, financial planner, or insurance agent for assistance.

If your spouse set up a pension plan prior to 1984, he may have elected, without your consent, to leave no survivor benefits in order to be entitled to the maximum pension benefits during his lifetime. On plans set up since 1984, federal law requires that the spouse's notarized signature appear on the document to signify that she has waived survivor's benefits or that she chose an amount less than 55 percent of the spouse's payment.

Veterans' Benefits

If your spouse served in the military, call the Veterans Administration (VA) to learn whether you are entitled to survivor's benefits, other than funeral allowances. Call your local VA office (listed in the telephone directory under U.S. Government Offices). The Disabled American Veterans (DAV) and the Veterans of Foreign Wars (VFW) can also help you apply for benefits.

Individual Retirement Accounts (IRAs)

If you are uncertain whether your spouse had such an account, check income tax returns back through 1975. Your tax accountant, attorney, financial planner, or trust officer might know. Any of these individuals can guide you through the steps for transferring ownership of these accounts to your name or for collecting payments from them.

Keogh Plan

If your spouse was self-employed, he might have set aside retirement savings in a Keogh Plan. The company bookkeeper, secretary, accountant, attorney, business partners, or associates may be able to help you track down the papers you need if you don't know where they are.

Deferred Compensation Plan

Check for this type of benefit in the same way you would an IRA or Keogh Plan. Individuals who earn a substantial income sometimes set part of it aside in investments to be used later as retirement income.

Annuities

Annuities are usually purchased through insurance companies and provide income to the policy holder or survivors. The income can be paid in regular monthly amounts or in a lump sum. Ask your insurance agent, your spouse's employer, or your accountant, attorney, or financial planner whether your spouse had such policies. Search carefully through all the papers, because people sometimes forget they have them. Ask questions before you throw anything anyway.

Dealing with Problems

Here is a set of procedures to use if you have complaints about how your questions or claim are being handled.

- Ask to speak with the supervisor of the person with whom you have the problem.
- If you disagree with the interpretation of a policy or pension document, consult an insurance agent for another opinion.
- Ask your attorney to check the matter for you. If necessary, call the Legal Aid Society for a referral to low-cost legal services.
- Contact the DOL's Pension and Welfare Benefits Administration for help with complaints against private companies. Your local DOL office can put you in touch with the nearest regional office.
- If you cannot get satisfactory results by going through the chains of command at the DOL or the Veterans Administration, contact your Congressional representative's office for help.

28

USING THE SERVICES
OF YOUR BANK

Banks can provide valuable assistance in settling final
details after the death of a loved one. Here are some
tips to help you make the best use of their services,
both immediately and over the long run.

- If you need funds from the deceased's account but
  are not a joint owner, ask whether the bank has on
  file a "payable on death" form authorizing you to
  withdraw funds. Under some circumstances, banks
  will release funds if you present a copy of the death
  certificate.
- Set up an estate account to receive funds earned by
  the deceased before his death. You can use this account to pay bills on behalf of the estate. To do this,
  you will need a separate taxpayer identification number, which you can get from the U.S. Internal Revenue Service. If you have an accountant, lawyer, or
  financial advisor, she can help you obtain the necessary number.
- Open an account in your name and use it to deposit
  your survivor's benefits checks.
- Change accounts you held jointly with the deceased
  to your name. You might need a copy of the death
  certificate to do this.
- Check the contents of the safe deposit box for insurance policies, a copy of the will, and other important
  records. If the deceased rented it in his name alone,
  you may remove only the will and other papers per-
  taining to the death. The remaining contents will be
  released after the will has been probated. Some states

allow you continued access to the box if your name appears on the rental agreement.

- If the deceased had loans from the bank, ask whether they were insured. You will need the account numbers to do this.
- Authors Charlotte Foehner and Carol Cozart suggest in *The Widow's Handbook* that you ". . . ask your bank what financial and estate settlement services they offer. Many banks have trust departments that can administer property from an estate."

Here are some tips for making efficient, economical use of bank services as you rebuild your life after a loss. If you change banks, be sure that your new one insures its customers' money through the Federal Deposit Insurance Corporation (FDIC). This coverage insures all accounts under your name in the same bank for up to $100,000. If you have more than $100,000 and want to put it into one bank, open more than one account. Limit the balance in each one to $100,000, and put them under slightly different ownership. For example, you could put $100,000 into a joint account in your name and your daughter's name and then, in a second account, deposit $100,000 in your name and your son's name. Your entire $200,000 will then be insured.

If you have accounts in your name only and you want a survivor to have access to the funds in the event of your death, name that person in a "Payable on Death" form.

Investigate how you can get the most service for the least cost. For example, many banks offer free checking if you have a savings account at the same institution or keep a minimum balance in your checking account. On some accounts, you may write a certain number of checks free each month and pay a fee for each additional one. You should keep enough in your checking account to cover your necessities and to qualify for economical banking services and put the rest of your funds into other types of accounts and investments that earn higher interest.

Banks offer a number of services that can simplify your financial management. For safety and convenience, you might consider automatic deposit of Social Security, pension, or investment dividend checks into your checking account. You can also authorize your insurance carrier(s) and mortgage company to withdraw their monthly payments directly from your account. In addition, many banks will pay certain monthly bills, such as telephone, light and heat, or credit card balances, from your account, and some will balance your checkbook for you. (There is usually a fee for these services.)

Ask if your bank offers carbonless checks, which allow you to record each check automatically on the slip behind it as you write the original. This can save you many frantic moments in the early months of grief when it's easy to forget to record checks in a separate register, making it harder to keep track of your finances.

Ask about bank-by-mail and telephone transfer of funds. These services can be convenient when you're in a pinch for time or if transportation is a problem.

Finally, check with your bank if you need referrals to accountants, financial planners, realtors, real estate appraisers, or attorneys in your community.

29

FINDING AND USING LEGAL SERVICES

If your current attorney is the same one who tended the affairs of the deceased, you can use his services in a number of ways. From the day you notify him of the death, he can guide you through the steps necessary to resolve the final details. For example, he can:

- Assist you in locating the will and other necessary documents.
- File the will with the court.
- Help you settle the estate if the deceased died without a valid will (intestate).
- Advise you of your options if you think the will is unfair to you. However, it is important to note that if you want to contest the will, it's in your best interest to engage an attorney *other* than the one who drafted it. ". . . Your lawyer's abilities and loyalty to you become very critical," write Foehner and Cozart in *The Widow's Handbook.*
- Guide you in carrying out your responsibilities as personal representative of the deceased or executor of the will.
- Help you determine whether you are eligible for survivor's benefits from pension plans and insurance policies and file the claims.
- Help you transfer ownership of automobiles, insurance policies, property, or investments.
- Refer you to other professionals whose services can make your life easier, such as, real estate brokers, mediators, financial planners, accountants, and real estate appraisers.

When a death changes your financial, legal, or care-giving responsibilities, an attorney can help you to restructure your affairs by:

- Changing or drafting your will.
- Drafting a living will.
- Writing a Durable Power of Attorney.
- Informing you about various types of trusts and offering advice about which ones could be useful to you.
- Helping you to specify your wishes for the care of your dependents, such as aged, disabled, or mentally incompetent family members or grandchildren, in the event of your death.

"Your attorney should have experience in estate administration (most lawyers do not) and should know how to deal with the property transfers, tax problems and human issues that often accompany the death of a loved one. An experienced probate lawyer is familiar with the territory," according to Foehner and Cozart. Your family lawyer may or may not have the skills you need at this time. Ask him to refer you to an attorney who specializes in estates and probate if he can't help you.

If you need to find an attorney, use these sources to get referrals:

- Word-of-mouth from friends who have used similar services.
- Your local bar association.
- Telephone book under the listings for Attorneys and Attorneys' Referral & Information Services.
- Your local probate court.

Use these questions to interview several attorneys before making your selection:

- Will you schedule an initial consultation at no fee?
- How much experience have you had in cases similar to mine?
- What do you charge for a case such as mine? Some

attorneys charge by the hour, others work on a flat rate basis, and still others take a percentage of the estate (the average is four percent). In her book *A Survivor's Manual To: Contingency Planning, Wills, Trusts, Guidelines for Guardians, Getting Through Probate, Taxes, Life Insurance,* author Charlotte Kirsch warns survivors that a percentage charge is best only for large or highly complicated estates.

- Will you give me a written estimate of your fee for handling my case?
- May I have references regarding your professional services?

If you have complaints about the service you are, or are not, receiving from your attorney—for example, phone calls unreturned, vague explanations, cost overruns, delays in settlement of the case—contact the grievance board of your local bar association or the consumer protection agency in your community.

Consider the following alternatives for legal services if you have a low income:

- The Legal Aid Society. Check the telephone directory for an office in your region.
- Legal Services Corporation (LSC), a federal service for low-income individuals. Contact the headquarters for the location of an office near you. Write to the LSC at 400 Virginia Avenue SW, Washington, D.C. 20024-2751; (202) 863-1820.
- Ask your local bar association about low-cost or "pro bono" legal services in your area.
- If there is a law school in your community, ask whether it sponsors a legal clinic offering low-cost or free services.

30

FINDING AND USING
THE SERVICES
OF AN ACCOUNTANT

Look to your accountant for tax information and guidance, but don't assume that she is familiar with the specialized field of estate taxes. Ask her whether she is experienced in estate settlement, or whom she recommends for this work.

If you must search for an accountant, be sure to select a certified public accountant (CPA). Request the following information to help make a sound choice.

- Professional credentials
- Written estimate of the cost to settle the estate
- The names of three references for whom she has done estate settlements.
- If the Internal Revenue Service inquires about the returns, ask whether she will meet with you and the agent or complete the required forms.
- Ask how she would coordinate services with your attorney and financial planner, if applicable.

Financial columnist Jane Bryant Quinn advises in *Everyone's Money Book,* ". . . choose a firm that is open for business all year round, so that if a question comes up about your tax return, you can get help."

An accountant can provide the following services:

- Prepare the final income tax return for the deceased.
- Pay fiduciary taxes (taxes due on income that accrues to the estate before it is settled).

- Cooperate with your attorney in preparing the tax return for the estate.
- Provide year-round tax advice.

Other Sources of Tax Assistance

Although you can use the services of public accountants to prepare routine tax returns, you may find that you need a more highly skilled accountant, a CPA, to handle a complicated estate. Your need for a CPA will depend on the complexity of the deceased's financial affairs.

Your attorney may also be able to assist you with the tax forms involved in estate settlement, but may charge you more than an accountant.

Commercial tax preparers who work with large income tax preparation companies are qualified to prepare simple income tax returns, but are not the best sources of help for estate settlements.

The U.S. Internal Revenue Service (IRS) and the American Association of Retired Persons (AARP) together offer free tax counseling and help older adults complete tax forms. Call either your local IRS office or the AARP chapter for help in your community.

Write down the dates, topic of discussion, and follow-up agreements for all conversations with your accountant or whoever helps you with tax matters. These records will be helpful to both of you when questions come up in the future.

If you have problems with your accountant that you cannot resolve directly, Foehner and Cozart suggest the following courses of action: Contact the state board of certified public accountants if the person is a CPA, or the Internal Revenue Service, the Better Business Bureau, or the consumer affairs office of your city, county, or state government if the person is not a CPA.

31

DO YOU NEED A FINANCIAL ADVISOR?

Giving financial advice is now a profession and is not to be confused with off-the-cuff opinions from an insurance agent or your second cousin who did well in real estate. Today you can expect sound advice from trained professionals on how to make money work for you.

Here are a few reasons you might consider using the services of a professional financial advisor:

- You are now solely responsible for managing your financial affairs and want to do it competently.
- Your financial affairs are more complex because of the recent death.
- You want professional advice in determining whether your assets will meet your short- and long-term needs. You might want to work with a professional on a temporary basis or engage her services regularly.
- You want to hone your money management skills, learning the latest opinions and resources so you can effectively manage your own finances in the future.
- You choose to delegate the task of overseeing your financial affairs to a knowledgeable professional.
- You want professional guidance in making investments.

You can find financial advisors in brokerage firms, in bank trust departments, in companies that manage the assets of individuals and organizations, and in self-owned businesses. Financial advisors can be stockbrokers, trust officers, registered investment advisors, asset management advisors, or certified financial planners.

They each have different kinds of training and credentials.

Foehner and Cozart suggest that you have the following information available before meeting with a financial advisor:
- Your assets and liabilities, monthly expenses and income, current investments
- Immediate and future cash needs
- Income needs from your current investments

You should also assess your tolerance for uncertainty and risk in financial investments before you actually sit down to discuss alternatives; you'll save time and effort if you already know the level of unpredictability you can or will accept.

If you think it would be helpful to work with a financial advisor, either temporarily or on a regular basis, check the next key for information on choosing a professional to suit your situation.

32

CHOOSING A FINANCIAL ADVISOR

Before you choose a financial advisor, you should determine the type of financial advice you need. Do you need
- Investment advice?
- An effective plan for managing your assets?
- General consultation on your financial affairs?
- Estate planning assistance?
- Assistance in settling an estate for which you are executor?

Here is a list of several types of financial advisors and the services they provide:

Registered stockbrokers. Stockbrokers must pass an exam to qualify to buy and sell stocks and bonds on customers' orders. Stockbrokers work either for full-service brokerage firms or at discount brokerages. Discount brokers serve investors who want to place buy and sell orders without the advice and background information that full-service firms provide, and accordingly charge lower commissions.

Bank trust officers. Bank trust officers have training in financial management and legal issues. Often they are attorneys. Trust officers can assist with estate planning and settlement. They are qualified to design and administer trusts and can help with some tax and real estate matters. Their fees are based on the value of the assets they manage for you; some of their services, such as selling property, carry extra fees.

Certified Financial Planners (CFP). A certified financial planner must pass the qualification requirements of the International Board of Standards and Practices for Certified Financial Planners, Inc. (IBCFP). The IBCFP recommends that Certified Financial Planners be investment advisors registered with the Securities Exchange Commission (see below). A CFP can help you to "evaluate how much you have to invest, and . . . decide how much and whether to invest in stocks, bonds, life insurance, mutual funds, savings or retirement plans," write Foehner and Cozart.

Registered Investment Advisor (RIA). A registered investment advisor is a person who deals with stocks and bonds. RIAs can be stockbrokers or certified financial planners. To become an RIA, an individual must file a registration with the U.S. Securities and Exchange Commission (SEC).

Financial advisors charge fees on the following bases:
- Hourly rate
- Flat fees for specific services, for instance, designing a plan to protect your nest egg while earning interest income
- Commissions from the sale of financial products, including stocks, bonds, insurance, real estate partnerships, and mutual funds
- A percentage of the total value of your assets (CFPs often use this approach)

Stockbrokers and insurance agents usually make their livelihood from commissions on their sales. CFPs are most likely to charge hourly rates or a percentage of your assets (the percentage charge is common for continuing management of sizeable assets). Some advisors work on a combined flat-rate-plus-commission basis. In these cases they usually earn commissions on the financial products they sell you.

Beware of free services or low-cost fees, warns financial columnist Merle Dowd. Since financial advisors have to make a living somehow, they often follow up their suggested plans by advising you to buy insurance or investments on which they do make commissions.

Those CFPs who charge only for their planning services can usually refer you to other professionals who will sell you the insurance or investments you need to meet your financial goals.

To find a financial advisor, start with word-of-mouth referrals from your friends, attorney, bank trust officer, or accountant. Check the names through the SEC, your consumer protection agency, and the Better Business Bureau to see whether complaints have been lodged against them. Then interview several advisors before selecting one. The following questions can elicit useful information as you screen candidates:

- What training and credentials do you have?
- How long have you been doing this work?
- How are you compensated for your services?
- Will you provide the names of three people as references?
- Will you give me a written estimate of what you would charge if I were your client?

You should also ask yourself if there is mutual respect and if you would be comfortable working with the person.

An ethical financial advisor will explain the degrees of risk connected with any financial move you contemplate. He will expect you to be candid about your tolerance for risk in light of the possible financial gain. Steer clear of anyone who badgers you or makes outlandish claims for returns on potential investments.

If you have problems with your financial advisor, contact the SEC if the person is a Registered Investment Advisor or stockbroker. If you are working with a CFP, contact the IBCFP, 1660 Lincoln Street, Suite 3050, Denver, Colorado 80264; (303) 830-7543.

33

THE LIVING WILL: WHAT IT CAN AND CANNOT DO

Grief too often carries the painful memory of a loved one kept alive after dignity was lost. Having a Living Will is one way to protect your dignity through the end of your life.

Within limits, Living Wills are effective legal documents. At this writing, 40 states and the District of Columbia recognize them as legally binding, although their powers and limitations vary from state to state. Here is a general description of the uses and limitations of the Living Will:

- The person must be diagnosed as having a terminal illness in the medical sense. This does not include debilitating strokes or Alzheimer's disease. Medical opinion varies on whether multiple sclerosis, Parkinson's disease, and amytrophic lateral sclerosis (Lou Gehrig's disease) are terminal illnesses.
- If a person is clearly in the last stages of life because of heart disease or diabetes, for example, but not in a "persistent vegetative state," the Living Will does not apply.
- When a person is rendered incapable of communicating by an accident, the Living Will does *not* protect him from being revived and kept alive.
- Living Wills often come into effect after the person is in a coma a certain number of days, during which time treatment expenses can soar.
- Often there are restrictions on who may serve as a

legitimate witness in signing a Living Will. Some states exclude people who, in a court of law, would have any claim or expectancy of property from the patient's estate.

- The question of whether and when artificial nourishment comes under the governance of a patient's Living Will is hotly debated—and still unresolved.
- Some states allow family members to challenge a Living Will in court even if its conditions are met.

You can use the following measures to strengthen the effect of your Living Will, and thus your control over how you spend the last stages of your life.

- Learn how the Living Will operates under the laws of your state. For more information, contact your attorney, your regional memorial society, which is listed in the telephone book under Funeral Pre-Arrangements, or the Society for the Right To Die, 250 W. 57 Street, New York, NY, 10107, (212) 246-6973.
- Discuss your wishes and concerns about end-of-life decisions with your family, friends, physician, and attorney.
- If you choose to have a Living Will, give a copy of it to your family, friends, physician, and attorney.
- Consider whether you will be serving your best interest by using a pre-written Living Will or by drafting one with the help of your attorney. If you don't have an attorney, choose one for this task who is familiar with older adults and their concerns.
- Ask two people you know and trust to function as surrogates who will make decisions, or at least voice your wishes, if you become incompetent. You need to name two surrogates so that if one is unavailable in a crisis, the other can act for you.

The next Key offers information about the Durable Health Care Power of Attorney, an important if not essential adjunct to the Living Will.

34

THE DURABLE
HEALTH CARE
POWER OF ATTORNEY

The Durable Health Care Power of Attorney (DHCPA) is an essential companion to the Living Will. It is wider reaching and more flexible, but not a substitute for, the Living Will. With a DHCPA you may designate an *agent* to act on your behalf if you become unable to make decisions for yourself. You can specify the conditions under which you should be considered unable to make decisions.

The DHCPA allows you to spell out your preferences for treatment of problems which the Living Will does not cover, including Parkinson's disease, Alzheimer's disease, heart disease, disabling strokes, AIDS, dementia, persistent vegetative states, coma, amytrophic lateral sclerosis (Lou Gehrig's disease), or multiple sclerosis.

Through your DHCPA you can explain what you mean by generalities such as "death with dignity" or "quality of life." For one person, death with dignity may mean that she wants heavy doses of pain control medications even if it shortens her life, whereas someone else might want to use her own discretion about the timing and amount of pain medications. Another person might consider his dignity compromised if he had to depend on others for transportation; for another, dignity would be lost if he could no longer feed himself. This should all be spelled out in your DHCPA.

Your DHCPA can explain your preferences regarding nursing home or in-home care, artificial nourishment and hydration, artificial life support measures, kidney dialysis, experimental drugs or medical procedures, and organ transplants. You can even arrange for the care of your pets if you are incapacitated.

The "trail map" model for DHCPA, which is written by an attorney with your consultation, is preferable to pre-printed or fill-in-the blank models. It reflects your personal values, preferences, and circumstances and conforms to the laws of your state. Having one drawn up can cost several hundred dollars; some families consider this guidance from their older relatives an invaluable gift and will share the expense.

Having a DHCPA offers these advantages:
- Minimizes family confusion and conflict
- Can protect your physician from legal risk
- Protects you from unwanted, costly medical treatment and prolongation of life
- Gives your agent clear guidelines on how to carry out your wishes
- Gives you a measure of control over how you spend the last stages of your life

Since the DHCPA is a personal document that has the potential to shape some of the most important events of your life, think about it and talk it over with your family, friends, spiritual or religious counselor, and physician.

If you choose to have your DHCPA drafted by an attorney, find one who is sensitive and knowledgeable about the ethics and legalities of health care issues for older adults. DHCPAs are part of the emerging field of "elder law," and your family attorney may not have the knowledge to do a quality job in this instance. To find qualified lawyers:

- Contact your state or local bar association. Ask if it has an Elder Law Committee and get the names of two or three members if it does.
- Contact estate-planning law firms and talk with attorneys who work on health-care planning issues for older adults.
- Contact the National Academy of Elder Law Attorneys, 655 N. Alvernon Way, Suite 108, Tucson, AZ 85711; (602) 881-4005 for the names of attorneys in your area.

See Key 29 for questions to ask an attorney.

A knowledgeable attorney will know which questions to ask you and how to draft the documents efficiently. Some attorneys charge by the hour for services of this kind; others base their fees on the amount they would theoretically save you by preventing unnecessary hospitalization or costly medical procedures. Since one day in a hospital's intensive care unit can run as much as $2,500, this type of fee can result in a higher expense than a per-hour rate.

When your DHCPA is finished, give copies to your family, agent, physician, and family attorney.

35

PROTECTING YOUR ASSETS FOR THE SHORT TERM

As a survivor, you must cope not only with your emotional loss, but with the pressure of managing money in lump sums. If you are accustomed to this, you at least have experience to rely on. If not, it's essential that you develop some basic skills.

During the intense stages of grief, it helps if you can preserve some order in your life by tending to immediate necessities. This will keep a rein on the anxiety or fear you might feel as a normal part of grief. As you recover, you'll be better able to muster the strength and clarity of mind to manage your assets for the long term.

Here are some basic guidelines for short-term protection of your assets.

Make a list of all your assets.
- Your job earnings
- Your personal assets or survivor's benefits from: pension, Keogh, Individual Retirement Accounts (IRA), Social Security, annuity, profit-sharing plans
- Cash in checking or savings accounts, certificates of deposit (CDs) or money market accounts, survivors benefits from insurance policies, the deceased's final paycheck and unused sick pay or vacation pay, cash value in life insurance policies, savings bonds, money owed to you or the deceased
- Your home, equity in your home, other real estate
- The value of your business or that of the deceased

- Investments: stocks, bonds, mutual funds, government securities, limited partnerships, or others
- Personal property: cars, household furnishings, art, jewelry, collector's items, tools, sporting equipment

List all your liabilities.
- Outstanding bills for medical care, nursing home or in-home care, medications, funeral expenses, estate settlement fees
- Mortgage on your home or other property
- Auto and bank loans, loans against insurance policies, credit card balances, personal or business loans, installment loans, liens against your property or business, back taxes
- Insurance premiums
- Monthly living expenses, including food, utilities, transportation, clothing, medications, personal home health care, property taxes

Make a budget.
Having a budget will help you weather the forgetfulness and confusion you may experience during mourning. A budget is a particularly important tool if you are not accustomed to managing finances or if your financial picture changed significantly when you lost your loved one.
- Track your expenditures and income by making simple notes each day. Put these in the notebook you use to record telephone conversations and other daily activities. If you save your receipts, be sure to note what you bought because you won't remember three or four days later. Record the amount and source of incoming checks as soon as you open them.
- Get a household budget notebook from a drugstore or stationery store. Fill in your estimated and actual income and expenditures for several months. If you

need to cut expenses, or if you are better off than you expected, you will have solid facts on which to plan.

Understand the options you have in paying your bills.
If you are concerned about having enough to pay off debts such as medical bills, funeral expenses, or bank loans, don't panic—but don't ignore your creditors, either. "When debtors clam up, collection efforts grow more severe," writes financial columnist Jane Bryant Quinn in *Everyone's Money Book*. Even when the invoices demand full payment upon receipt, most creditors will negotiate a payment plan. Write a letter or make a phone call and explain your circumstances. Tell the creditor you want to work out a plan to pay a certain amount each month. If you need to skip a loan payment or reduce payments while you get on your feet, contact your creditor and make the arrangements. Most of them prefer this to collection procedures.

Get help if you need it.
Whether you need to learn basic money management skills, change your spending habits, or wade through reams of paperwork, you don't have to do it yourself. Ask for help from your trust officer, accountant, or financial advisor. Otherwise, consider hiring a financial planner or advisor for three to six hours to help you make a plan to protect your assets until you recover from the intense stage of grief. Nonprofit credit counseling agencies also provide free help with budgeting and debt repayment programs. Contact the National Foundation for Consumer Credit, 8701 Georgia Avenue, Suite 507, Silver Springs, MD 20910. Call (800) 388-2227 and give your long distance area code to get the name of the credit counseling agency in your area, or call (301) 589-5600 for general information.

Protect yourself from hasty decisions and frauds.

Lump sum death benefits are a favorite prey of con artists. (For further details on protecting yourself from frauds, see Key 24.) Resist making investments, extending loans, and buying "bargains" for a year or two after the death. Put your money into low-risk, interest-bearing accounts at a bank insured by the Federal Deposit Insurance Corporation (FDIC).

Protect yourself with basic insurance.

• Medical Insurance

If you were covered under your spouse's group policy, you can continue that coverage for up to three years if you arrange for it and pay the entire cost of premiums yourself. This is often cheaper than buying individual health insurance. Contact the insurance company or your spouse's employer for information.

Another option is to purchase your own group coverage. Sometimes this is less expensive than staying with your spouse's group. The following organizations offer group policies: The American Association of Retired Persons (AARP), 1909 K Street, NW, Washington, D.C. 20049; (202) 872-4700; National Council of Jewish Women, 53 W. 23 Street, New York, NY 10010; (212) 645-4048 (women of any denomination may join); Co-op America, 2100 M Street, NW, Suite 403, Washington, D.C. 20063, (800) 424-2667.

If you are within three months of age 65, or older, and are eligible for Social Security, you may apply for Medicare. There is usually no premium for the hospital insurance (Part A). If you are not eligible for the free Medicare hospital insurance, you can purchase it if you are 65 or over. For the medical services insurance (Part B), there is a monthly premium, which is low compared to other insurance. You may want to consider a supplemental insurance policy (sometimes called "medi-gap" insurance) to cover the services Medicare excludes.

For Medicare application procedures and for consumer guidelines on shopping for medigap insurance, contact your local Social Security Administration office. Ask for the free pamphlets "Your Medicare Handbook" and "Guide to Health Insurance for People with Medicare."

• Long-Term Care Insurance

Since Medicare and other medical insurance policies provide almost no coverage for in-home or nursing home care for long-term illnesses, it's in your best interest to provide this protection for yourself.

Sit tight for one to two years.
Give yourself time to heal before making long-term decisions about finances, living arrangements, or personal commitments.

36

DECIDING WHEN AND WHETHER TO MOVE

The most common advice concerning moving is to wait a year before you make any decisions. Heed this advice, if possible, because grief can temporarily cloud your capacity to make sound long-term decisions and can deplete your physical strength, as well. Immediate concerns such as filing insurance claims, paying bills, and setting the estate can usurp much of the time and energy you would need for sorting, packing, and preparing your home for sale or rental.

On the other hand, it may not be practical for you to stay where you are if your income is sharply reduced or if your physical condition makes it impossible for you to live alone. As a temporary alternative, consider in-home assistance. If your house is isolated, being closer to others may afford peace of mind and contact with others that can help you recover from your loss.

If and when you decide that a move is in your best interest, remember the following considerations and cautions:

• Think carefully before agreeing to list your property with a friend or relative; it's hard to mix personal and business relationships. Politely decline offers from friends or relatives to handle the transaction for a reduced commission, the natural inclination is to relegate such "courtesy" listings to the bottom of the priorities list. If, in the end, you do choose to list with a friend or relative, insist that the commission and terms of the sale be the same as those you would establish with any qualified realtor. This will give both parties the rights and responsibilities of a legitimate business transaction and will protect your personal relationship from misunderstandings and failed expectations.

- Beware of an agent who offers to "buy your listing" and promises to get you a higher selling price than other agents. This is a maneuver to get the listing; agents know that most properties ultimately sell at their fair market value. Insist that your property be put into the Multiple Listing Service (MLS) to ensure that it gets maximum exposure to potential buyers.
- As you look for an agent to handle your sale, keep in mind that someone who sells properties in your vicinity is likely to have a realistic knowledge of the property values. An agent who works close by can be more attentive to your needs as a client than someone who does most of his business in another part of town.

In planning where you will move, take these considerations into account:

- Think things through carefully before you decide to move closer to your adult children or other relatives. Although such a move works well for some, for others it's disappointing. One advantage of such a move is the possibility of mutual assistance among family members. If, on the other hand, there are long-standing frictions, chances are that they will surface under the stress of loss and change.
- If you move closer to your family recognize that, while they might welcome you, they already have their own activities, obligations, and friends. So you may find yourself in the temporary or permanent status of outsider to their established routines. Remember that your adult children may not have contacts that will lead you to friendships with those your age.
- Family members of your own age may have access to those your own age, medical care, church groups, or

112

volunteer work, but these may not be compatible with *your* needs and preferences.

- Be prepared to take the initiative in adjusting to your new home, and accept the help your family extends if it is useful.
- Many people value their familiar surroundings, neighbors, and church over the conveniences of easy transportation or proximity to family.

If you move, the kind of living arrangement you choose will influence your adjustment and comfort. A wide range of options is available.

Living arrangements exclusively for older adults range from modest, high-rise apartment buildings to developments resembling plush resorts. Often they have staff who assist with daily living activities, for example, administering medications, bathing, and dressing. One attractive feature for many individuals is the meals served in central dining rooms. Transportation for shopping, medical care, and entertainment is often available.

Living and storage space in such accommodations are usually limited. This can be an advantage if you don't require spacious living quarters, but a disadvantage if you enjoy puttering in a workshop or a garden, if you need extra space for your pets, or if you like to cook and entertain on a large scale.

Your preferences regarding privacy and the proximity of neighbors also affect your choice of dwellings. For example, apartment living brings close proximity to neighbors. For some people, this is a welcome opportunity for friendships, whereas for others it's a threat to privacy.

Do you enjoy living around people of various ages, or would you rather live close to others in your age group? Apartments, single-family homes, condominiums, and townhomes afford more contact with people of various ages, while older-adult residences provide neighbors who are on average 60 years old and older.

In deciding whether, or when, to move after you lose a loved one, ask yourself if the effort of moving and adjusting to a new home outweighs the advantages you expect to gain. Think about your ease or difficulty in adjusting to change in the past. Remember that a new living situation could be even more difficult because you have so many changes to absorb.

37

CULTIVATING YOUR SUPPORT NETWORK

As you climb out of the depths of grief, you'll feel a stir of readiness to embrace life once again. If you had friends who stood by you through the sorrow, perhaps you feel less need for their ministrations now. If the support you wanted was absent, perhaps you are wondering how you can build it now so you'll have it if you need it in the future.

This key suggests actions you can take to cultivate your existing network of support or to develop a broader one. The word "cultivate" is purposely chosen to describe this activity because it involves a two-way process of investing effort and reaping the rewards.

As you emerge from your grief, perhaps you'll want to let others know this and extend your appreciation for their support. Find ways that suit your temperament and style; here are a few examples.

One widower wrote notes and called friends and relatives throughout the thirteenth month after his wife died. He said it was like taking off the black armband to let the world know that he was through the worst part of his grief. He thanked them for their support and asked them to let him help when they needed anything.

Consider calling friends who listened kindly as you poured out your grief. Express your appreciation and ask them to update you on what's going on in their lives.

One widow held a tea for her friends, church members, and fellow volunteers. She thanked them for their kindness and ended her remarks with a rollicking tale about the misadventure she and her late husband Jerry had when they cooked lobsters the first time. Then she told them, "Don't be afraid to talk about Jerry around me. Remember I belong to his fan club, too."

If you have friends or relatives living out of town, strengthen your bonds with them through letters. Explain how you've come to appreciate the importance of keeping strong ties with the people you love. Keep your correspondence short and newsy. If you have difficulty writing your thoughts down, clip articles or cartoons from the newspaper and enclose them with a brief "thinking of you" message. Make use of the new greeting cards which convey messages of friendship and caring.

Here are a few thoughts on building a support network:

- Different relationships offer different gifts; no single one is complete or perfect. Some people bring laughter, some give quiet dependability, some stimulate your mind, some bring comfort in times of trouble, some help you organize and get things done. Others help you to feel loved, share your interests, help you see life in ways you usually don't look at it, bring easy companionship, or share memories of times past. Fill your life with a variety of people, and value what each one contributes to your support network.
- Cultivate ties with people of different ages outside of your family circle.
- Be prepared to participate in mutual sharing if you want to have a strong, reliable network of support.
- If your self-confidence is hurting and you are wondering why anyone would be interested in you, remember that interest, acceptance, and kindness toward others are bound to attract people who could eventually become your friends.

116

- Sometimes the greatest gift you can give to another is a listening ear and empathy: "This must be difficult for you," or "I'm so pleased for you." Advice seldom enriches friendship unless it's issued sparingly upon request.
- Use the telephone as a way to cultivate your network. If you call to chat for a while, ask first whether your timing is convenient. For example, you could say, "Good morning, Harriet. I called to say I'm thinking of you and to catch up on things. Is this a convenient time to talk for a while?" Allow give and take in your conversation rather than directing all the attention to your own concerns.
- Keep your calls short so your friends won't feel trapped when they hear your voice. By the same token, let others know when your time is limited. Say, for example, "I just have a minute this evening, but may I call you around 4 tomorrow?"
- Relationships thrive on appreciation. When someone does something for you, acknowledge it. Gestures of appreciation can be as varied and creative as you wish—a two-minute phone call, a postcard, a single rose, a set of theater tickets, a gift certificate, an invitation to lunch, or an offer of transportation to a friend for a morning's errands are a few examples. Sometimes it isn't possible to return a favor directly to the giver. In those cases, think about how you can do something for someone else in honor of that generosity. It's a way to give something back to the human treasury for what you received.

38

GETTING THE MOST
FROM YOUR TIME

You don't *have* to do everything you think you *should* do. Here's a way to free yourself from the tyrannical *shoulds* so you can tend to the things that make your life worthwhile. Time management consultant Alan Lakein calls it the "ABC Priority System."

First, make a list of the things that are clamoring for your attention. Don't judge their importance; just write them down. Your list many include, for instance, vacuuming the upholstery in your car, getting a restful night's sleep, filing an insurance claim, and signing up for a class.

Second, look over your list and measure the importance or value of each item. For instance:
- It's important to my personal safety.
- My physical health depends on it.
- It's two months overdue.
- It keeps me awake at nights.
- I have an agreement to do it.
- I've promised myself I'd do it for five weeks but it isn't essential.
- It's bugging me to distraction.
- Others are counting on me.
- It's a convenient diversion from other activities that would truly please me.
- I need the money.
- It makes me happy.
- I do it because I don't like to change old habits.
- It would increase my peace of mind.
- I would save time and aggravation in the long run.

- I do it because others might think ill of me if I didn't.
- I feel worthwhile when I do it.

Next, assign each item a priority, "A," "B," or "C." This is how you can sort your *shoulds* into *I Will Dos* (either now or later) and *I Won't Dos.*

Your priorities will change from day to day. Jot down an ABC list every day on a sheet of paper divided into three columns. Yesterday's "B" may become today's "A" because of an approaching deadline. Today's "A" may become a "C" in a couple of days as you figure out an alternative solution to the problem. Depend on written lists, rather than mental ones, Lakein advises, in *How to Get Control of Your Time and Your Life.* "Why clutter your mind with things that can be written down? It's much better to leave your mind free for creative pursuits."

Don't overwhelm yourself with good intentions like "settle the estate," "start getting some fun out of life," "find a job," or "get organized." Instead, list the small steps by which you can accomplish these goals. For example, one day's A list could consist of:
- Call the accountant to ask when estate tax forms will be ready for signature.
- Call Marge to set up movie date.
- Tell Barney Watkins I'm available to work 15 hours a week.
- Buy a box of file holders.

As you assign priorities to various activities, be aware that 80 percent of the benefits will come from 20 percent of the items on your ABC list. This is the 80/20 rule. Lakein gives this example: "Eighty percent of the reading time is spent on twenty percent of the pages in the newspaper (front page, sports page, editorials, columnists, feature page)."

Use the 80/20 rule as you decide which items merit most of your time and energy. Let your values and circumstances be your guide. At one point, having peace of mind may be more important than risking disapproval if you turn down a major volunteer assignment. At another point in your life, the comfort of old habits may be more important than following strict health measures.

Only you can decide what you most want from your time. Using the methods we've described can help you move from wish to reality. Lakein writes, "There is always enough time for the important things. The busiest people are able to find time for what they want to do, not because they have any more time than others, but because they think in terms of 'making' time by careful scheduling."

39

FINDING FULFILLING ACTIVITIES

Here is a tool for exploring your interests, your dreams, and your passions. Once you have a clear view of them, you can pursue them through activities that will give meaning and purpose to the next chapter of your life.

To start, spend two minutes on each of the following questions. Write your answers on a sheet of paper or mull them over in your mind.

Question #1 If I had $10 million, tax-free, to spend any way I chose, I would . . .

Question #2 In the past I sometimes daydreamed that if I did not have to work for a living, did not have family obligations, or had more time, I would . . .

Question #3 This world would be a better place if . . .

Question 1 deals with an imaginary resource; few people actually have that much money at their disposal. But your answer holds clues to how you might use the resources you do have to put greater meaning and satisfaction in your life.

One of your resources is time—24 hours or 1440 minutes each day. As you spend that nonreplaceable resource each day, how often do you arrange to get something you value in return?

One way to establish a sense of control over your time is to resist the temptation to say, "I don't have time." The fact is you do have time—1440 minutes each day. Say instead, "I have time. I choose not to use it that way."

Often people say that if they had $10 million they would contribute large sums to their favorite charity. One woman who answered this question realized that she could become a benefactor to her favorite charity simply by spending portions of her time on volunteer work. With that insight, her volunteer service became far more than busy work and took on major significance in her life.

Maybe you would use some of your mythical $10 million for travel; however, in reality, you have precious few dollars left after you pay your bills each month. Maybe you have untapped resources of skill and energy that could be your keys to travel opportunities. For example, some people become tour guides for nonprofit organizations or businesses; they travel free. Others put their skills and energy to use in part-time jobs and save every spare penny for travel.

The results of spending your resources of time, energy, and skill, may be less spectacular than if you spent $10 million, but they can enrich your life nonetheless.

Question 2 challenges you to take a fresh look at your long-held dreams. Don't squash them with excuses: "I'm too old, too rusty, too clumsy, too uneducated, too . . ." There are many different paths to every destination, and different ways to realize any dream. For example, a woman who worked for decades as a seamstress and typist but who always dreamed of being on stage became a professional clown at the age of 65. An auto mechanic who dreamed of being a teacher finally started his teaching career at age 66 when he taught basic auto maintenance and repair to a group of teenagers from his church.

Answering question 3, did you feel your pulse quicken as you thought about what would make the world a better place? Whether your passion concerns political reform, cleaning the litter in your neighborhood, or stopping child abuse, there's a way to do something about it and make the world a better place in the process. You might channel your efforts through a volunteer organization devoted to the purpose, through paid employment that serves the cause, or private action on your own.

Two widows in an urban neighborhood, for example, bemoaned the collection of litter in their block as they took their daily walk together. They agreed to start carrying trash bags and picking up as much as they could on each walk. "It was good exercise, too," one of them laughed. Their action started a wave of improvements in the block, less vandalism, better communication among the residents, and a babysitting co-op.

By acting on their passions about making the world a better place, many people put meaning into their own lives and deepen their sense of self-worth. If you want to explore the possibilities of working through volunteer service organizations to make the world a better place, check the information in Key 43.

If, after reading this Key, you've decided to chart a course of action that will deepen the meaning and joy in your life, be sure to write down the first step on your A List for today (See Key 38), even if that step is as elementary as looking up a phone number.

40

FINDING NEW FRIENDS THROUGH COMMUNITY GROUPS

As you recover from your loss, you will face the challenge of growing beyond the boundaries of the person you were in the past. You can meet this challenge by giving the relationship with your loved one an honored place in your history as you stretch to embrace values and interests that will shape your future.

One way to do this is to expand your circle of friends through community groups. This can enrich your life in two ways: First, you'll find opportunities to pursue existing interests or develop new ones, and, second, you'll meet people who share your interests—a natural setup for friendship! If you question how this could work, recall how you met the people who are now your friends. How many of them date back to volunteer service, military duty, professional interests, hobbies, or jobs?

As you think about community groups, consider the array of possibilities open to you. Here are a few ideas to pique your imagination.
• Groups Based on Special Interests
• Classes (as a student or teacher)
• Volunteer Work
(Please refer to Key 43 for more information about volunteer service.)

Use techniques including the following to get better acquainted with people who belong to the same group as you:

- Host a small gathering at your home or apartment. If you serve food, keep it simple or make it a potluck meal. Show a videotape related to the group's common interest. Have a study session or a planning meeting. Gather for a special television program with coffee and discussion afterward.
- Ask a member of the group to join you for a cup of coffee after a meeting.
- Invite a group member to sign up with you for a tour related to your common interest.
- If you particularly enjoyed associating with an individual during a project, tell her so and ask whether she would like to get together in the future. If the answer is affirmative, be sure to take the lead in arranging your first get-together.
- Don't let shyness rob you of the pleasure of new friendships. Remember that you're in the company of thousands of people who are uncomfortable or downright scared in new situations. Calm yourself by using some of the techniques explained in Key 15. It's also perfectly acceptable to admit that you're a bit squeamish. For example, you could say, "This is all new to me. For many years, I stuck pretty close to the same old routine." Quite often you'll find that others are complimented by your interest in them, and you'll be on your way to the next step—deciding whether you want to build a friendship or leave it a pleasant acquaintance.

41

USING PERSONAL ADS TO WIDEN YOUR SOCIAL CIRCLE

Personal ads used to be the province of lonely hearts and people of dubious intent. Today, however, men and women of traditional values and excellent character use "personals" or "person-to-person ads" to meet others of similar interests and values. Here are some of their reasons:

- Dissatisfaction with current opportunities for meeting people
- The desire to check out potential friends or companions before actually meeting them
- Interest in new experiences and adventures

If you decide to use a personal ad, follow these four steps.

Identify what you're looking for.

- Friends or companions of the same sex, opposite sex, either sex?
- A fellow enthusiast to share a hobby, interest, activity, or sport—doll making, Revolutionary War history, folk dancing, or canoeing, for example?
- A companion for a one-time event such as a visit to a music festival?
- Long-term or short-term romance with a person of the opposite or same sex?

Shop for the best spot for your ad. The following suggestions were made by the editor of a weekly paper and by several people who have used personal ads.

- Find a publication that targets the readers you want to reach. Personal ads appear in daily newspapers, shoppers, special interest and professional magazines, and alternative newspapers found outside libraries, supermarkets, restaurants, or entryways to shopping malls. Some papers have "Golden Singles" or "50-Plus" sections. Some of the publications aimed at older adults also carry personal ads. Read as many papers or magazines as you can find to see which ones best match your personality and expectations.
- Protect your privacy. Check out the publication's procedures for accepting reader responses. Make sure that the paper protects the identities of clients who place ads. If you notice that the ads list names or personal phone numbers, you might want to steer clear of that paper. Some publications have elaborate systems of identication codes and central phone numbers through which clients first connect with respondents; others accept only written responses and give those to the clients. Even if you pay extra for such services, it's preferable to publishing your personal mailing address.

Write your ad.
- Look at the style of ads in the paper you've chosen. See what appeals to you, then be creative. If you fall victim to writer's block, ask a friend to help you out.
- Be straightforward about what you want. This gives you and your respondents the best chance of making a satisfactory match. It's appropriate to specify your preferences regarding drinking or smoking habits, age range, height and weight, religious preference, marital status, family ties, level of physical fitness, racial background, gender, educational level, and anything else that's important to you. When you describe yourself, ". . . everything you say should be true. You

might as well admit you're a couch potato if that's so rather than saying you love to cross-country ski," according to a woman who used personal ads before she met her husband-to-be. Another woman says, "I wanted to meet a Jewish man and I said so. I didn't want to have to teach him what a bagel is, and I didn't want a Christmas tree in my house!"

- One woman who received both phone and letter responses believes she got the best results with the latter. "I can learn a lot more about a person by what they say and how they say it on paper than I can from a phone conversation," she claims. If you prefer written responses to phone calls, say so.

Answer your respondents.
- "It's best to meet on neutral ground, like a restaurant, for the first time or so," says one man. "That way, no last names or phone numbers have to be exchanged unless you want to. If it turns out to be tedious, you can say thanks and go your separate ways."
- This advice from an editor who handles personal ads: "Be a little guarded at first, especially if you are widowed. Don't pour your heart out when you write letters to your respondents or when you talk to them on the phone until you get to know them. [At our paper] we do the best job we can to screen callers before we connect them with our clients, but you can still get taken if you're not prudent."
- As a matter of courtesy, answer all responses even if it's just a postcard that says, "Thanks, I'm not interested at this time."
- "Even if you don't find what you're looking for, you can have fun and meet some interesting people," says a woman who advertised for a ballroom dance partner and ended up with a job as assistant to an agent who booked dance bands.

128

42

FINDING A JOB

A job can be an important part of rebuilding your life after a major loss. It can help you structure your time productively, meet people, earn income for necessities or a few luxuries, and master new challenges.

If you fear that doors will be closed because of your age, it may come as a surprise to you that many employers will want to hire you because of your maturity. They know that you are likely to bring reliability, sound work habits, and good judgment to a job. For instance, the 44-year-old supervisor of a garden center was enthusiastic about having a 70-year-old woman join the staff. "Priscilla went out of her way to learn things," the supervisor said. "She had great patience in answering customer questions. And her grace in dealing with the difficult customers was a lesson to all of us!"

As a job-seeker, you have an astounding array of opportunities if you've gotten off the ladder of "success" where every job must carry prestige and promotional possibilities. When you're off that ladder, you're free to pursue the offbeat subjects of your curiosity—bookstores, florist shops, the circus, the zoo, a newspaper, and . . . (add yours to the list).

Use the following steps to find or create job opportunities:

Know Yourself.
Do your homework. Don't depend on prospective employers' imaginations—use yours. Decide what you can—and want to—offer in the workplace. Then help that future employer understand how you can use your

skills to make her life easier. Start with this quick skills identification.

Select your first, second, and third preferences: Working with:
• people
• information/ideas
• objects/things

Choose your favorite skills in working with:

People: Taking instructions, helping, persuading, amusing, supervising, leading, advising, counseling, or training.

Information/ideas: Observing, comparing, filing and retrieving, computing, researching, analyzing, organizing, evaluating, improving, adapting, creating, or planning.

Objects/things: Working with the earth and nature, working with machines or tools, being athletic, operating vehicles, or repairing.

Make notes to yourself about your preferences and desires in the following aspects of work:
• Work schedule
• physical surroundings
• geographic location of the job
• types of co-workers
• level of responsibility
• self-employment or on payroll
• level of pay

Write your resume.

This will be valuable whether or not you ever show it to anyone. It will help you to organize your thinking and speak confidently about your assets.

A functional resume highlighting the skills you're currently offering will serve you best. This, rather than a historical account of your past experience, is the information prospective employers want.

When you finish the four preceding steps, you've done your homework. Now it's time to go public.

Make connections.

Tell *everyone* you know that you are available to make some employer's life easier. Everyone includes:

- friends and acquaintances
- former bosses and co-workers
- doctor, dentist, attorney, accountant, banker, financial advisor, barber, hairdresser
- pastor, rabbi, church or synagogue members
- club members
- support group or therapy group members
- relatives
- everyone else you meet

Remember, you're not asking for favors. You're looking for that employer who needs the skills you have to offer. As you talk with people about your interest in a job, explain what skills you are marketing; give copies of your resume freely. Ask people for the names of individuals and organizations who might be looking for those skills.

Consider other ways of finding a job. Volunteer positions or internships, for example, often lead to jobs in for-profit as well as nonprofit organizations. See Key 43 for more information. Temporary jobs can also open doors to interesting experiences as well as long-term work. The director of one temporary service actively seeks older adults to fill a variety of openings. She says, "Employers want the wisdom and judgment that older workers have. But most importantly, mature men and women are *there* when the employer needs them."

Check available resources. Sources of information include:

- *Working Options—How to Plan Your Job Search, Your Work Life* (Order number D12403), American Association of Retired Persons (AARP) Fulfillment, 1909 K Street, NW, Washington, D.C. 20049.
- Temporary help services in the telephone directory under Employment Contractors-Temporary Help.
- Local libraries, social service agencies, museums, parks departments, tourist attractions, cultural centers, fire and police departments for interesting volunteer positions with employment potential.
- Albert Myers' *Success Over Sixty: How To Plan It, How To Have It, How To Live It* (New York: Summit Books, 1984) for how-tos and many real life examples of successful employment.
- Nancy Olsen's *Starting a Mini-Business: A Complete Guide to Starting a Low-Risk, Part-Time, Home Business* (Sunnyvale, CA: Fair Oaks Publishing, 1988) for practical, low-cost tips on self-employment.
- Richard Bolles' *The Quick Job Hunting Map* (Berkeley: Ten Speed Press, 1985) for a guide to identifying your skills and finding a job.
- Tom Jackson's *The Perfect Resume* (New York: Doubleday, 1990) for a workbook guide to writing a functional resume.

43

FINDING MEANINGFUL VOLUNTEER WORK

Any volunteer job can have two faces. To one person, it's pleasure and inspiration; to the next, it's as dull as a plate of mashed potatoes and soft boiled turnips. Why? Because the job matches the first person's interests, skills, energies, curiosities, or needs but is all wrong for the second person.

Here are four tips for successfully matching your volunteer efforts with needs in your community. When something grabs your interest, check it out or find a similar opportunity in your area.

Focus your attention on subjects that intrigue you. For example:
- Old trains and railroads
- Supporting the performing arts
- Helping frail elders maintain their homes
- Guiding crime victims and witnesses through the courts
- Preventing family violence
- Planning quality programming through public television and radio
- Promoting self-help in Third World countries

Identify a talent, skill, or interest that you love to indulge. When you find a way to do that as a volunteer, you have a formula for satisfaction.
- Enriching life for nursing home residents
- Bringing history to life
- Being out of doors

Decide which personal rewards you want for your volunteer service. You can look for, or arrange, these rewards as you seek or create your volunteer niche.

- Learning new skills
- Feeling worthwhile
- Meeting other people
- Traveling
- Adventuring
- Keeping physically fit
- Learning about job openings
- Fulfilling a dream
- Keeping a sharp mind

Physical impairments may cramp your style but not necessarily your volunteer spirit. "If I can't be involved one way, I'll do it another," says a woman who is legally blind and dependent on a wheel chair and walker. She makes daily telephone reassurance and social calls to homebound or isolated persons in her community. Other volunteer possibilities include computer operation, tutoring, peer counseling, and teaching reading and math skills.

Look. Ask. Suggest.

- After narrowing down the type of work you want to do, check out or initiate opportunities. For national and international opportunities, check Mary Kouri's *Volunteerism and Older Adults* (Santa Barbara: ABC-Clio, 1990) or the current edition of *Volunteer! The Comprehensive Guide to Voluntary Service in the U.S. and Abroad* (New York: Council on International Educational Exchange).
- Do more than ask whether an organization needs volunteers. Ask, "Do you need a volunteer to *(fill in this blank with the skills and competencies you wish to contribute)*?"

44

TRAVEL: OPTIONS UNLIMITED

"Whatever you thought you knew about travel ten years ago is irrelevant today," says travel writer Allison St. Claire. The world is closer than you think. Opportunities abound for *experiencing* the world, rather than just seeing it. Here are a few examples:

- You can tour 2200 miles of Alpine roads on a motorcycle, stopping in villages and feasting your eyes on the wonders along the way. If you prefer to go by auto, you can arrange that. Contact Alpine Autours; 14 Forest Avenue; Caldwell, NJ 07006; (201) 226-9107 or (800) 443-7519.

- There are thousands of recreational vehicle (RV) devotees who travel in groups to destinations like the Rose Bowl or the Olympics. They also tour foreign locations in RV caravans. Contact Loners of America, Route Two, Box 85E, Ellsinore, MO 63937; (314) 322-5548, or Loners on Wheels, P.O. Box 1355-CM, Poplar Bluff, MO 63901; (314) 785-2420.

- If you thrive on vigorous activity, you can join the Over the Hill Ski Gang. Their motto: "Once you're over the hill you pick up speed." Contact 13791 E. Rice Place, Aurora, CO 80015; (303) 699-6404. Outward Bound U.S.A. provides wilderness experiences to challenge and exhilarate people of all ages and physical conditions. Contact 384 Field Point Road, Greenwich, CT 06830; (203) 661-0797 or (800) 243-8520.

- Through volunteer vacations, you can travel (at your own expense) to U.S. and foreign locations that you might not see on commercial tours and participate in service projects during your stay. See Bill McMillon's *Volunteer Vacations: A Directory of Short-Term Adventures that Will Benefit You . . . and Others,* 2nd ed. Chicago: Chicago Review Press, 1989.
- Specialized tours are now available to meet any interest imaginable. You can visit bonsai gardens in Japan, a battlefield where you fought as a World War II soldier, or communities where you think you might settle down in retirement.

There are several points to consider about traveling alone. First, you don't have to travel alone even if you don't have a companion waiting in the wings. Second, it can be more interesting to travel alone than with a companion. Third, if you want a companion, you don't have to settle for a boring one. Fourth, you can have the best of both worlds if you plan it cleverly. Read on for details.

- There are numerous groups and tours that cater to the solo traveler. Some of them are formed around common interests and activities; others are for seekers of romance.
- Traveling alone does have its advantages, writes Frances Weaver, traveler and author, in *Last Year I Went Around the World . . . This Year I Plan to Go Elsewhere,* "In case of necessary change of plans, you won't waste half a day saying, 'Well, I don't care. What do *you* want to do?'" She points out.
- Many people travel with their grandchildren or other young relatives. Intergenerational tours are quite common.
- Plan your trip so you can meet prospective companions when you arrive. For example, stay at bed and

breakfasts; choose a topic that interests you and attend a conference related to it; visit a pen pal. Sign up for an Elderhostel class. (See the Appendix for contact information.)

Can you afford to travel? Probably so, especially if you're resourceful.

For international travel, according to St. Claire, "You can literally go to the dock as a cruise ship prepares to set sail, offer $400.00 for a room, and if they have an empty one, they'll probably take your offer. They have to sail whether that room is filled or not, and they like to have all the paying passengers they can get, even at discount rates." Check the classified ads in your newspaper for discounted airline and cruise tickets from brokers or private parties.

A competent travel agent can open all kinds of doors to pleasant, affordable travel. Keep your schedule flexible and ask her to notify you about bargains on air fares and to keep you up-to-date on see-the-USA travel packages on buses and trains.

45

WHETHER OR WHEN
TO REMARRY?

Fulfillment in a marriage or permanent relationship starts with recognizing your hopes and expectations for it. Any of the following are possible reasons for wanting to remarry or to build a long-term relationship with a mate of the same or opposite sex:
• to share companionship and sex
• to have someone to look after you
• to share expenses
• to have someone who needs you
• to have someone who loves you
• to have a "special person" or a "significant other"

Any of these is a legitimate expectation as long as you are clear and candid with the other person. With "all the cards on the table," both parties can make responsible choices and agreements. It's the partial truths, the assumptions, and confusion about what you really want that pave the way to disappointment. Splendid relationships can blossom amid the oddest circumstances, leaving the casual observer to wonder how in the world people could be happy "living like that!" The answer is that they're happy because both parties are satisfied with the mutual give-and-take.

Here are a few opinions and observations about remarriage and recommitment from different viewpoints:
• One grief counselor cautions that when you think about a commitment with someone who has lost a loved one, "Consider whether your prospective mate has grieved. Otherwise, the grieving process takes

place within the context of the new relationship and that causes problems."

- A woman in her late 60s shares this insight from her observations of many bereaved friends and family members: "Men seem to need a woman to help them grieve."

- Marion Pease Davis wrote in Berman's *The Courage To Grow Old,* of her husband's death after a 47-year marriage, "As with grass, new love naturally fills the empty spaces left by a lost partner. This does not diminish the first love, but rather honors it by saying: 'My life with you was so great that, now that it is over, I need another strong love with which to fill the emptiness that losing you has left within me.'"

- A woman who remarried after the death of her first husband, divorced a year later, and married again ten years later shared this: "Remarry according to your needs—social, financial, personal, or spiritual. But, as with everything else when you suffer a loss, take your time. You might think you're finished grieving when you're not."

To smooth the way toward a harmonious relationship:

- Draw up a prenuptial agreement to protect the assets of both parties and to ensure that the assets pass to your survivors according to your wishes. You will need an attorney's help with this.

- Discuss with your prospective mate how you will divide your day-to-day living expenses.

- Discuss your wishes regarding end-of-life choices. Make sure your Living Will and Durable Health Care Power of Attorney are current.

- Air your mutual desires about how to handle family gatherings and holidays.

- If you want to learn whether you are compatible before stepping into a permanent relationship, consider living together for a while first.

Remarriage is not always possible or practical, but that does not have to rule out a loving commitment to a mate. If you both have limited incomes, for example, you might not be able to make ends meet on the Social Security payments you would receive as a married couple. Many people in this position share their lives by living together. If one of you has a marriage or prior commitment to a partner devastated by Alzheimer's disease, you might choose to share a new relationship while honoring your earlier commitment. Davis describes her relationship with a man whose wife suffered from Alzheimer's disease: "If the fates are kind, we may have a few happy years ahead in marriage together. If the fates are unkind, his wife will linger, having already lived on past her own happiness. Or one of us may die too soon. If we were able to get married now, we would, for we'd like to respect the mores of our culture. But whatever happens, at least we have made the end of our lives more comfortable, more exciting, more fun, and more filled with love."

QUESTIONS AND ANSWERS

Q. My husband died ten months ago and I still have no interest in social activities or travel which I used to love. Will I ever feel like my old self again?

A. Each person recovers from grief in his or her own way and time. The circumstances of your husband's death, the nature of your relationship, and your own coping style all affect your readiness to build the next phase of your life. It may take a year or two before you'll be ready to reinvest your energies in old or new interests.

Q. I've been so forgetful since my wife died. I'm concerned about my mental state, and my children are concerned, too. Do other people have memory problems like this after they lose a family member?

A. Temporary forgetfulness often accompanies the physical and mental stress of grief. Ease your concern with memory aids such as lists and notes to yourself.

Q. After my son died of alcoholism, my friends gave me the cold shoulder. How can I make them understand that I loved him and have a right to my grief?

A. Losing a child is among the most painful of human experiences. Consider joining a support group where you can find the acceptance and solace you need to recover from your pain. It's a frustrating fact of life that people have virtually no control over their friends' opinions or actions.

Q. Would it be best to move to the town where my children live now that my husband is gone?

A. If possible, wait for one or two years before making such a major change. If you have close friends and fulfilling activites in your present location, your grief might worsen if you leave them behind. On the other hand, if you don't have close friends or absorbing interests, being near your children may provide a measure of comfort.

Q. After my husband died, I refused to take tranquilizers, but now I am exhausted from lack of sleep. Is there some medication I can use without getting hooked?

A. Talk with your physician about a mild sleep medication. If you decide to use one, use it sparingly—once a week, for example, or the night before an activity for which you particularly want to be rested.

Q. I've always had good health and took care of my wife at home through the last months of her life. Now I get colds and viruses, my gums are sore, I have digestive problems, and I'm tired all the time. What can I do to get my health back?

A. The events you have been through would deplete anybody's physical and emotional reserves. See your doctor for a check-up. Make sure that your foods are nutritious, exercise moderately, get enough rest, and arrange for the emotional support you need. Be patient with yourself; it may take several months for you to regain your good health.

Q. I don't want to burden my friends or husband, but I can't seem to get over my sister's death. We were very close. What can I do?

A. Many people find help through support groups.

Check with churches, hospitals, or hospices in your community to locate one.

Q. My mother died two years ago, and I just found a life insurance policy in a box of her old papers. Is it too late to collect the death benefit?

A. Chances are that you can still collect the proceeds if you put your request in writing and enclose a death certificate with your letter to the insurance company.

Q. I heard that Social Security pays for funeral expenses. Who is eligible for this?

A. Widows and widowers of persons who had Social Security benefits are usually entitled to a death benefit of $255. You must submit the claim within two years of the death.

Q. My mother is getting threatening letters on loans she did not know my father made before his death. She's afraid she'll lose her home unless she borrows money to pay the creditors. What can she do?

A. First verify that the loans were actually made. If they were, see whether they were insured. If your mother is actually responsible for the debts, the non-profit consumer credit counseling agency in her vicinity can help her work out a repayment plan with the creditors. Call (800) 388-2227 for the location of a center near her.

Q. I feel betrayed because my married friends stopped inviting me to social events after my husband died. Is it common for married people to drop their widowed friends?

A. Unfortunately your experience is similar to that of many widowed persons. It might be in your best interest to develop some new social involvements with single adults. Explore such avenues as volunteer work, educational programs, singles groups, or employment.

Q. My husband and I enjoyed a wonderful, loving marriage until he died after a short illness. Although I miss him terribly, I have not suffered from paralyzing grief like some of my friends did when their husbands died. Am I cold-hearted?

A. If you were capable of participating in a loving marriage, you undoubtedly have a warm heart. Often when couples share deep love and respect but maintain full lives as separate individuals, they can cope with the loss of a mate without being devastated.

GLOSSARY

Anticipatory grief The sad, angry, or fearful feelings that arise when a person learns of the impending death of a loved one.

Death benefit Cash payments to survivors from insurance policies, pensions, and other sources after a death occurs.

Death certificate The legal document that certifies that an individual has died. This paper is necessary in most financial and legal transactions concerning the affairs of the deceased.

Durable health care power of attorney A legal document in which a person specifies his or her wishes regarding health and personal care decisions should he or she become unable to make such decisions. This document names the person who should act on behalf of the disabled person.

Final details Burial arrangements and the legal, financial, and business matters that must be settled after an individual's death.

Financial advisor A professional who can assist with financial affairs such as investments, decisions regarding insurance purchases, or retirement planning. A financial advisor can be a stock broker, bank trust officer, registered investment advisor, asset management advisor, or certified financial planner.

Grief support group Regular meetings of individuals who help each other recover from the pain of personal loss.

Living Will A legal document in which an individual states his or her wishes regarding the use of medical treatment and life support measures in the event of certain extreme illnesses or disabilities. The applicability of the Living Will varies according to the laws of each state.

Personal ads Short advertisements through which individuals seek others to share common interests or mutual activities. Sometimes called "personals," these ads usually appear in the classified sections of newspapers and other publications.

Travel agent A professional who assists with travel arrangements, including itinerary planning, making reservations for transportation, lodging, tours, and car rentals, and locating the most economical fares for various modes of travel. Most agents work for travel agencies and do not charge customers for their services.

Unfinished business Issues in a relationship that remain unsettled at the death of one of the parties.

APPENDIX—CHECKLIST
A "TO DO" LIST FOR
THE FIRST TWO YEARS

This key suggests lists of necessary tasks and a time frame for completing final administrative, financial, and legal matters during the first two years after the death of a loved one. It also offers tips for maintaining your personal well-being during this period.

Second to Third Months
- Apply for survivor's benefits from Social Security, the Veterans Administration, the deceased's retirement plan, Keogh plans, Individual Retirement Accounts (IRAs), accidental death policies, group life insurance policies, and annuities. Be sure to photocopy all paperwork before sending it out.
- Consider whether to hire an accountant, attorney, or financial advisor to help settle the estate.
- Determine whether there is insurance on the mortgage, auto loan, bank loans, or credit card balances.
- Make a short-term budget. A household budget notebook from a stationery store may be helpful. List outstanding bills—first, the regular ones such as heat, light, telephone, mortgage, rent, loan, or car payments; then list health and other insurance premiums. Next, add the one-time bills such as medical bills for the deceased, funeral expenses, and travel costs in connection with the funeral. Determine what assets are readily available, such as checking accounts, saving accounts, money market accounts, life insurance

147

benefits, investment income, and the deceased's final paycheck.
- Pay the bills as your assets allow. If the money is tight, call creditors and arrange for installments.
- Make sure your auto insurance is in force.
- Check that your driver's license is current. If it's up for renewal this year, note it on your calendar.

Fourth through Sixth Months
- Review whether your present assets and income can sustain your present level of expenditures.
- Assess your emotional well-being. Would it be helpful to join a grief support group or seek other assistance at this stage of mourning?

Seventh through Ninth Months
- Attend to routine property maintenance to avoid headaches and expenses later. If you have a car, change the oil and filter, check the brakes and the coolant and antifreeze levels, rotate the tires, and check the tread. If you live in a cold climate, disconnect garden hoses in the fall to keep the pipes from freezing and rupturing, get the furnace cleaned and checked by a reputable person, and put up the storm windows.
- Review your physical and spiritual well-being. Are you eating nutritious foods, getting adequate vitamins and minerals, drinking eight glasses of water a day, exercising and sleeping regularly? Take a few minutes each day for meditation, prayer, inspirational reading or listening to tapes, relaxation exercises, or writing in your journal.
- Consider your needs for insurance for long-term care, a Living Will, and Durable Health Care Power of Attorney as protection for yourself and your survivors.

Tenth through Twelfth Months

- Complete the estate settlement.
- Start to rebuild your social life.
- Look into volunteer service or a paid job if you don't have such involvements.

Thirteenth through Eighteenth Months

- Evaluate your investments to determine whether they suit your present circumstances.
- Review and adjust your budget based on your experience in the past 12 months.
- Consider whether your living arrangements match your current needs and preferences.

Ninteenth through Twenty-fourth Months

- Think about freshening up your home with new paint on the walls, new upholstery and cushions for your favorite chair, or a new reading light. Perhaps it's time to lighten your maintenance responsibilities by installing a sprinkler system for your lawn.

RESOURCES FOR UNDERSTANDING GRIEF

Books and Audio Tapes

Brooks, Anne M. *The Grieving Time: A Year's Account of Recovery from Loss.* New York: Dial Press/ Doubleday, 1985.

Caine, Lynn. *A Helpful Guide to the Problems of Being a Widow.* New York: Arbor House, 1988.

Gordon, Beverly S. *The First Year Alone.* Dublin, NH: Wm. L. Bauhan, 1986.

Grollman, Earl A. *Time Remembered: A Journal for Survivors.* Boston: Beacon Press, 1987.

————, ed. *What Helped Me when My Loved One Died.* Boston: Beacon Press, 1981.

Hewett, John H. *After Suicide.* Philadelphia: Westminster, 1980.

Kushner, Harold S. *When Bad Things Happen to Good People.* New York: Avon, 1981. Also on audio tape: Warner Audio.

Lord, Janice H. *No Time for Goodbyes: Coping with Sorrow, Anger and Injustice after a Tragic Death.* Ventura, CA: Pathfinder, 1990.

Matthews, Jack. "The Last Abandonment," pp. 138-153 in Abrahams, William, ed. *Prize Stories 1981: The O'Henry Awards.* Garden City, NY: Doubleday, 1981.

O'Connor, Nancy, Ph.D. *Letting Go with Love: The Grieving Process.* Tucson, AZ: LaMariposa, 1984.

Stearns, Ann Kaiser. *Living Through Personal Crisis.*

Audio Tape: Bantam Audio. (Also a book; see Bibliography for publication details.)

Westberg, Granger E. *Good Grief: A Constructive Approach to the Problem of Loss*. Philadelphia: Fortress, 1971 (Also in large-print edition.)

RESOURCES FOR MOVING THROUGH GRIEF

Books, Pamphlets, and Tapes

American Association of Retired Persons. *On Being Alone: AARP Guide for Widowed Persons.* Washington, DC: American Association of Retired Persons, 1988.

Bell, Lorna, R.N., and Eudora Seyfer. *Gentle Yoga: A Guide to Gentle Exercise.* Berkeley, CA: Celestial Arts, 1987.

Casey, Karen, and Martha Vanceburg. *The Promise of a New Day: A Book of Daily Meditations.* San Francisco: Harper & Row, 1983. Also on audio tape: Hazelden Cassette Library.

Estes, Clarissa. *The Radiant Coat: Myths and Stories on the Crossing between Life and Death.* (Audio Tape #A118) Boulder, CO: Sounds True, 1990.

Gagner, James, and Louise Hay. *Positively Yoga: The Body Mind Connection.* (Videotape) Hay House, 1988.

Gawain, Shakti. *Creative Visualization.* New York: Bantam Books, 1982.

Marshall, Catherine. *To Live Again.* New York: McGraw Hill, 1957.

Miller, Emmett E., M.D. *Easing Into Sleep.* Milwaukee: Music Design, 1981. (Audiotape)

Murphy, Jo. *More Alive.* Aurora, CO: Mature Adult Corporation, 1989. (Videotape).

Stearns, Ann Kaiser. *Coming Back: Rebuilding Lives after Crisis and Loss.* New York: Ballantine, 1988.

U.S. Department of Health & Human Services. *Depression.* Washington, DC: Alcohol, Drug Abuse, and Mental Health Administration, 1990.

Organizations

Alcoholics Anonymous (AA)
P.O. Box 459
Grand Central Station
New York, NY 10163
(212) 686-1100

Al-Anon
P.O. Box 862
Midtown Station
New York, NY 10018-0862
(800) 356-9996
(212) 302-7240

American Association of Suicidology
2459 S. Ash Street
Denver, CO 80222
(303) 692-0985

Hospice Education Institute
Five Essex Square
P.O. Box 713
Essex, CT 06426
(800) 331-1620
(203) 767-1620

RESOURCES FOR MANAGING FINANCIAL AND LEGAL MATTERS

Books and Pamphlets

American Association of Retired Persons. *Final Details: A Helpful Guide for Survivors When Death Occurs.* Washington, DC: American Association of Retired Persons, 1986.

American Association of Retired Persons. *Housing Options for Older Americans.* Washington, DC: American Association of Retired Persons, 1985.

Fullner, Wanda. *A Primer on Financial Management for Midlife and Older Women.* Washington, DC: American Association of Retired Persons, 1988.

Duff, Johnette, and George Truitt. *The Spousal Equivalent Handbook: A Legal and Financial Guide to Living Together.* Houston: Sunny Beach Publications, 1991.

Eisenberg, Ronni. *Organize Yourself!* New York: Collier Books, 1986.

Gillespie, Ann E., and Katrinka Smith Sloan. *Housing Options and Services for Older Adults.* Santa Barbara: ABC-Clio, 1990.

Magee, David S. *Everything Your Heirs Need to Know: Your Assets, Family History and Final Wishes.* Dearborn: Financial Publishing, 1991.

Porter, Sylvia. *Your Financial Security: Making Your Money Work at Every Stage of Your Life.* New York: Avon, 1987.

Organizations
Surviving Paperwork (After the Death of a Loved One)
1500 S. Zang Street
Lakewood, CO 80228
(303) 988-7498

RESOURCES FOR BUILDING THE NEXT CHAPTER OF YOUR LIFE

Books and Audio Tapes

American Association of Retired Persons. *Reminiscence: Finding Meaning in Memories*. Washington, DC: American Association of Retired Persons, 1989.

Hay, Louise L. *You Can Heal Your Life*. Santa Monica: Hay House, 1984.

Kennedy, Eugene. *On Being a Friend*. New York: Continuum, 1982.

Kouri, Mary K. *Elderlife: A Time To Give—A Time To Receive*. Denver: Human Growth & Development Associates, 1985.

Morgan, John S. *Getting a Job after 50*. Princeton: Petrocelli Books, 1987.

Moskowitz, Bette Ann. *Leaving Barney*. New York: Henry Holt, 1988. (Large-print edition available through Thorndike, 1988.)

Parr, Peggy. *Mountain High Mountain Rescue*. Golden, CO: Fulcrum, 1987.

Peck, M. Scott, M.D. *The Road Less Traveled: A New Psychology of Love, Traditional Values and Spiritual Growth*. New York: Simon and Schuster, 1978.

Rubin, Joyce Rhea. *Of a Certain Age: A Guide to Contemporary Fiction Featuring Older Adults*. Santa Barbara: ABC-Clio, 1990.

Schwartz, Lynne S. *Balancing Acts*. New York: Harper & Row, 1981 (paperback, 1983). (Large-print edition available through G. K. Hall, 1981.)

Stegner, Wallace. *Crossing to Safety*. New York: Random House, 1987 (paperback Penguin, 1988). (Large-print edition available through Thorndike, 1988, audio tape available through American Audio Prose Library, Braille edition, BR 07155, available through your local library, or National Library Service for the Blind and Physically Handicapped (202) 707-5100.)

Viorst, Judith. *Necessary Losses: The Loves, Illusions, Dependencies and Impossible Expectations that All of Us Have To Give Up in Order To Grow*. New York: Ballantine, 1987.

Organizations

Elderhostel, Inc.
80 Boylston Street
Suite 400
Boston, MA 02116
(617) 426-7788

Older Women's League (OWL)
730 Eleventh Street, NW
Suite 300
Washington, DC 20001
(202) 783-6686

Operation ABLE
180 N. Wabash Avenue
Chicago, IL 60601
(312) 782-7700 (job hotline)

BIBLIOGRAPHY

Phillip L. Berman, ed. *The Courage To Grow Old: Forty-One Prominent Men and Women Reflect on Growing Old, with the Wisdom and Experience that Comes from a Rich and Varied Life.* New York: Ballantine, 1989.

Alla Bozarth-Campbell, Ph.D. *Life Is Goodbye Life Is Hello: Grieving Well through All Kinds of Loss.* Minneapolis: Compcare, 1982, 2nd ed. 1986.

Caroline Bird. *The Good Years: Your Life in the Twenty-First Century.* New York: E. P. Dutton, 1983.

Scott Campbell and Phyllis Silverman, Ph.D. *Widower: When Men Are Left Alone.* New York: Prentice-Hall, 1987.

Merle E. Dowd. *A Consumer's Guide to Financial Planning: How To Get the Best Plan for Your Money.* New York: Franklin Watts, 1987.

Charlotte Foehner and Carol Cozart. *The Widow's Handbook: A Guide for Living.* Golden, Colorado: Fulcrum, 1988.

Charlotte Kirsch. *A Survivor's Manual To: Contingency Planning, Wills, Trusts, Guidelines for Guardians, Getting Through Probate, Taxes, Life Insurance.* New York: Anchor/Doubleday, 1981.

Alan Lakein. *How To Get Control of Your Time and Your Life.* New York: Signet, 1973.

Edna St. Vincent Millay. "At Least My Dear" from *Collected Poems,* Harper & Row. Copyright 1956, 1984 by Norma Millay Ellis. Reprinted by permission of Elizabeth Barnett, Literary Executor.

Jane Bryant Quinn. *Everyone's Money Book.* New York: Delacorte Press, 1978, 1979.

Therese A. Rando, Ph.D. *Grieving: How To Go On Living When Someone You Love Dies.* Lexington, MA: Lexington Books, 1988.

Harriet Sarnoff Schiff. *Living Through Mourning: Finding Comfort and Hope When a Loved One Has Died.* New York: Viking Penguin, 1986.

Stephen R. Shuchter. *Dimensions of Grief: Adjusting to the Death of a Spouse.* San Francisco: Jossey-Bass, 1986.

Ann Kaiser Stearns. *Living Through Personal Crisis.* Chicago: Thomas More Press, 1984.

Survivors. Baltimore: U.S. Department of Health and Human Services, Social Security Administration, SSA Publication No. 05-10084, January 1990.

Judy Tatelbaum. *The Courage to Grieve: Creative Living, Recovery, and Growth through Grief.* New York: Lippincott & Crowell, 1980.

Norma S. Upson. *When Someone You Love Is Dying: Sensitive, Timely Advice on Providing Primary Care for a Terminally Ill Loved One . . . from a Woman Who Faced this Challenge Herself.* New York: Simon & Schuster, 1986.

Frances Weaver. *Last Year I Went Around the World . . . This Year I Plan To Go Elsewhere.* Golden, CO: Fulcrum, 1989.

INDEX

Making the Most of Your Maturity With ...

Barron's Keys to Retirement Planning

Here are user-friendly manuals that offer advice on many aspects of mature living. Each presents an energized view of retirement, emphasizing its unique satisfactions. Each Key: Paperback: $5.95, Canada $7.95, 160 pp.

Keys To ...

Buying a Retirement Home Friedman & Harris (4476-2)

Choosing a Doctor Lobanov & Shepard-Lobanov (4621-8)

Dealing With the Loss of a Loved One Kouri (4676-5)

Fitness Over Fifty Murphy (4514-9)

Living With a Retired Husband Goodman (4705-2)

Nutrition Over Fifty Murphy (4512-2)

Planning for Long-term Custodial Care Ness (4593-9)

Preparing a Will Jurinski (4594-7)

Understanding Arthritis Vierck (4731-1)

Understanding Medicare Gaffney (4638-2)

Plus a comprehensive single volume of friendly general advice ...

Life Begins at 50: A Handbook for Creative Retirement Planning
by Leonard Hansen
Tips on retirement living, including handling your money prudently, knowing about available health care, Social Security and Medicare benefits, finding fun and bargains in travel and entertainment. Paperback: $11.95, Canada $15.95, 352 pp., (4329-4)

Barron's Educational Series, Inc.
250 Wireless Blvd., Hauppauge, N.Y. 11788
Canada: Georgetown Book Warehouse
34 Armstrong Ave., Georgetown, Ont. L7G 4R9

Prices subject to change without notice. Books may be purchased at your bookstore, or by mail from Barron's. Enclose check or money order for total amount plus sales tax where applicable and 10% for postage and handling (minimum charge of $1.75, Canada $2.00). ISBN PREFIX: 0-8120